Stories Behind Stances

Stories Behind Stances

Creating Empathy Through Hearing "The Other Side"

Chris Singleton

ConnectEDD Publishing
Hanover, Pennsylvania

This publication is available at discount pricing when purchased in quantity for educational purposes, promotions, or fundraisers. For inquiries and details, contact the publisher at: info@connecteddpublishing.com

Published by ConnectEDD Publishing LLC
Hanover, PA
www.connecteddpublishing.com

Cover Design: Kheila Dunkerly

Stories Behind Stances by Chris Singleton. —1st ed.
Paperback ISBN 979-8-9874184-2-0

ConnectEDD
PUBLISHING

Praise for *Stories Behind Stances*

Unity is a concept that often seems idealistic and unrealistic in a society that is polarizing and divided. The reason for this often lies in the fact that people have different perspectives and different stances about the issues we are forced to face each day. The brilliance of this book, *Stories Behind Stances,* is that it helps you see that every person has a story that shapes their stance and if we are simply willing to listen to peoples' stories and seek to understand and empathize, then we may realize that unity is not just a dream, but an actual outcome. Chris Singleton has delivered a treasure of a read and one that should be highly encouraged for people of all ages, all races, and all ethnicities; we will be better as a culture because of it.

—Brandon Bowers | Lead Pastor, Awaken Church, Charleston, SC

When I first met Chris a few years ago, I was struck with how mature he was for his age. Then, I listened to his story and understood why; he had to grow up faster than everyone else because of extreme adversity and tragedy. If you read this book with a mind that is open, ears to hear, and eyes to see, then you will get to know my friend, Chris Singleton.

—Damon West | Keynote Speaker and Wall Street Journal bestselling author of *The Coffee Bean*

I met Chris Singleton just hours after he lost his mother, and I have been impressed with him ever since. While I never got to meet his mom, I'll forever know exactly who she was because I see her strength in Chris with everything he does. This book is no exception, and its message is one from which we can all learn.

—Dan Linberg | Director/Producer ESPN

Chris is one of the most remarkable people I've ever had the privilege to profile. Since I met him, I've been in awe of his heart, his humanity, and his compassion. Reading this book allows you to see the world from the perspective of a person brave enough to look directly into the eyes of evil and offer forgiveness. This book will be a gift for anyone who seeks understanding over ignorance, unity over division and love over hate.

—David Gardner | Writer in *NY Times, Washington Post, Sports Illustrated*

Chris Singleton is an amazing inspiration with a life changing message! His unique genius in highlighting the range of views so common in a divided world, and most importantly how to build a bridge for a greater good, is so powerful and so needed. For all that choose to make a better world for their loved ones, their community, and themselves, this book and its messages can make an immediate impact—and build a better world united and aligned to see true potential realized. As one of our all-time most powerful speakers in fifteen years of Leadership Summits, this is one more gift from an amazing man who changes lives by the tens of thousands.

—Brad Black | President/CEO Humanex Ventures

I am pleased to say that I have had a personal connection with Chris since playing football with the Patriots back in 2014. Over the years, I have been impressed with his graceful and intentional transitions, as well as his ability to excel despite the challenges he has faced. Chris's mission to spread love and build unity has been a true inspiration to me.

Stories behind Stances is a powerful resource that has helped me and will help many others develop empathy and create a paradigm shift. I believe that it is an essential read for everyone who wants to grow personally and better understand the experiences of others. I am grateful to have had the opportunity to know Chris and to learn from his message of love and unity. I hope that more people will take the time to read *Stories behind Stances* and be inspired to build a better, more empathetic world.

—Shamiel Gary | Retired NFL Athlete, Author, and Speaker

I met Chris on June 10, 2017, while filming *Emanuel* in Charleston. He had just returned from his Chicago Cubs tryouts, and we were all hoping and praying for good news regarding his professional baseball career. Over the next six years I had the privilege of watching Chris grow as a son, husband, father, brother, Emanuel 9 family advocate, coveted public speaker, and award-winning author.

Chris is the quintessential humble warrior. His Spirit-led approach to life and honoring his parents and siblings by leading his family through unimaginable tragedy should be a lesson to us all. I am excited for Stories Behind Stances to be released and believe it will become an instant classic used by schools, community groups, and even businesses to increase their understanding and attunement regarding empathy through hearing what the "other side" has to say first.

—Dane Smith | Executive Producer, *Emanuel*

Table of Contents

Foreword

In today's world, we are constantly reminded of the divisions that exist among us. Whether it's political differences, religious beliefs, or cultural backgrounds, it's easy to feel as though we are living in a world that is increasingly polarized and unity is difficult to obtain.

But what if we could find a way to come together, to bridge the gaps between us, and to unite in our shared humanity? Ever since I have known Chris Singleton, he's been on a mission to unite people with love in order to counter hate and this book is a continuation of his relentless effort and goal to bring people of different beliefs together.

He shares the stories behind the stances of different people with different beliefs to remind readers that despite our differences, we all share a common bond as members of the human race. Chris explores various ways in which we can learn to see beyond our differences and embrace our shared values, hopes, and aspirations.

Through memorable and relatable stories and practical wisdom, Chris has crafted a guide that is accessible, inspiring, and thought-provoking for all. I love how he challenges us to examine our own beliefs and biases, to listen to those with whom we disagree, and to find common ground where we can work together to build a better world.

At a time when division and polarization seem to be the norm, this book is a much-needed reminder that by listening and understanding there is hope for unity. When we work together, we are able to overcome our differences and build a world that is inclusive, compassionate, and just.

Whether you're an educator, businessperson or simply a parent that wants to build a better world for your kids, I encourage you to read this book with an open mind and an open heart. May it inspire you to join in the effort to unite people of different beliefs, and to work towards a more united future for all.

– Jon Gordon, 14x best-selling author of *The Energy Bus* and *Power of Positive Leadership*

Introduction

A note to my parents:

Dad, what up, B?! I hope heaven is treating you well. Honestly, I don't visit your grave as much as I should. I'm sorry for that, but, deep down, I thought that after mom was taken away, you'd come in like a knight in shining armor and rescue us from the pain we felt. I want to apologize for the times that I was upset with you and said you didn't love us when in actuality you were really sick with your disease and couldn't shake it. Even though you're not here anymore, you taught me the important lesson to work through my pain or it may come back to haunt me in ways I don't want it to. I'm sorry for all the pain and trauma you endured as a kid, and I understand now. Despite all the pain you went through in life, I want you to know you were always a superhero to me. I mean, seriously, I do not know too many other dads who can be forty years old and only 6'2" tall and still do a drop-step dunk on 10 feet. You were so athletic and I'm praying for my sons to get some of their grandfather's crazy athleticism. I often talk about how I don't want to let my mom down, and sometimes people ask if I want to make you proud, too. The truth is, I already know I'm making you proud. You were on cloud nine after I was on the *Today Show* and your kids threw out the first pitch at a Yankees baseball game. I got us Pops–oh, and by the way, my first-born son's name is Chris, too. I had to keep it going. I love you B!

Mom, I wish you were here daily. It's funny to think about how you used to stress over writing your dissertation to become the first Dr. Singleton in the family. I now see why you were stressed. Writing this book has kicked my butt. I often get asked the question if I'd be doing the work I do if you were still here. The answer is simple: No. I would most likely still be chasing my baseball dream or be settled into my position as an athletic director at a high school. I also find it funny how you used to take Toastmasters classes to get better at speaking. Little did we know that I would be traveling the country 150 days a year speaking and keeping your memory alive. I hope I'm making you proud and I just want you to know that you did an amazing job as a mother. Caleb is thriving in playing baseball in college, just like me. He is still the smartest Singleton by far and I can't wait to see the man he continues to grow into. Camryn still has that fire that can't be dimmed. I smile thinking about the times you called your friends asking, "What am I about to do with this girl?" Well, she's grown up to be the fierce, loving, and caring woman we always knew she'd be. She loves people and cares about her family more than anyone I know. Thank you for everything, Mom. Sometimes at night when everyone's asleep, I'll pray over my family the same way you did for me growing up (minus that holy oil that would always run down my face, Ha Ha).

My parents raised me with love and care and if you are ever impressed with me, please know that it was my parents that made me who I am today. I believe in the power of teaching, and my parents did an amazing job teaching me to love and care for others. Since losing both of them, my mission for my life has been to spread love and unity through teaching and encouraging universal understanding around the world. Because of my parents, I have the strength and commitment that comes with dedicating my life to peace and harmony.

I also dedicate this book to everyone affected by hate crimes in the world. There is no place for hate and this book is written with the intent to stop them from occurring.

In this book we will be sharing life stories from both sides of various issues in the hope that these very controversial topics will be less divisive after you hear the other side. Again, unity isn't only when we all believe the same things; instead, unity is when we can agree or agree to disagree on whatever the topic is in a respectful manner.

As I sit here thinking about my hopes for this book, all I can think about is my mission of uniting families, businesses, and schools across the nation. This wasn't always my personal dream for my life. Serving as an ally for those who were feeling excluded and living in a more united world was something that I wanted, but I never thought that I would devote my life to this work. My dream as a kid was to play centerfield for the Yankees. I still remember the composition notebook where my mom and I wrote down my dream colleges I hoped to play for. I remember having to research all the stats that college players had in high school to make sure that I produced those numbers, if not better, to make sure I gave myself a shot to play just like them. Baseball was my dream and if that didn't work out, in the back of my mind I figured that I could be an athletic director at a local high school and have a beautiful life around sports while impacting the youth the same way that I was impacted. This was the life that I had planned for myself, but of course, that isn't the way things turned out.

Everything changed in Charleston, South Carolina on the night of June 17, 2015. It was on this night that the most unthinkable tragedy I could have ever imagined occurred. I lost a hero of mine. I lost my mother, Sharonda Coleman-Singleton. I didn't just lose her, but I lost nine Mother Emanuel AME Church family members in what was the most heinous act that the world had seen at the time. This awful act was committed by a 21-year-old self-proclaimed white supremacist with the intent to start a racial war. If this doesn't ring a bell yet, it's more commonly known as the Charleston Church Shooting, an event that was heard around the world, when a young man had so much hatred in his heart, that he fired over seventy bullets into our church, killing many instantly. The day after I lost my mother, two very important events took place in my life. One was a prayer vigil held at my high school and the school where my mother worked. I was asked by a BBC reporter how I felt about the killer, and I said, "We already forgive him." I vividly remember my little sister looking at me like I was crazy, but the words flowed out of my mouth as if there was something else guiding the words to come from my lips. The second event changed everything. I was at my college baseball field when many reporters showed up asking me questions and with nerves flowing I said, "Love is always stronger than hate, and if we just love the way my mom would, the hate won't be close to where love is." After saying this, the words went viral. I appeared on the *Today Show, ESPN E:60* and many other outlets and people wanted to hear more about what I thought we should do to unite our cities and do away with the hate that we see in the world.

I didn't know it at the time, but this was the start of what would be a fulfilling career and ministry that has changed many lives over the last eight years. Following the many nights of pain and heartbreak, I made a promise to myself and my mother that I would try to do the opposite of what this man tried to do. If he wanted to divide the world, I would commit my life to trying to unite the world and put an end to all the hate that we see on a daily basis. Currently, I'm on the road 150 days a year speaking to companies, schools, and organizations teaching the principles that I share in this book. What should you expect? When I thought about writing a book, I didn't want it to be another long treatise about race that nobody reads fully through. I wanted to make this book short, sweet, and to the point. After reading this book, I want people to work together to fix problems and love people regardless of their race, religion, or skin color.

In order for this book to do its job, I need you–all of you–to have enough courage to share your truth. So frequently in the work I do people will say, "Well, Chris, why do I, the oppressed, have to fix the problem? Why do I have to be loving? Why do I have to be the one to try to fix things?" I have learned over the last six years of my life, if we don't do things in a non-pugnacious, charitable way, we will never achieve the results we desire. So you must be willing to share the things that you've never shared. You have to put your pride aside and mostly love people who are different from you. Dr. King is someone in our history we celebrate for moving the needle more than many others have in the past and it is because, despite the fact that he didn't always think like those at the table, he knew he would have to share his truth and love those that thought differently than him. One of my favorite quotes to date from him is the following: "*Darkness cannot drive out darkness, only light can do that, hate cannot drive out hate, only love can do that.*"

Be open to sharing your story, because your great-grandparents likely weren't able to do so. If not for you, then for those that came before you.

My hope is that this book is used to bring people from all different walks of life to a place where they are able to agree to disagree respectfully through empathy and live in harmony. This book will present the story of people on opposing sides of many topics with a different perspective for the first time. My intent is that by learning the story behind the other side's stance, it will instill in readers a new level of empathy. After reading this book, you will have a better understanding of what unity looks like, you'll be able to respectfully agree or agree to disagree with others, and you'll be equipped to be the change that you wish to see in the world. More than anything, though, I hope that by writing this book I'll make my mom and dad proud.

Author's Note

Parents, it's time that we all take a look in the mirror. I travel all across the world learning from the next generation and I've seen tons of studies done related to how our children are responding to the world after missing vital time in school during the pandemic. What I have personally noticed is that for the last seven years, there has been a "lack of respect" problem. Now, I'm not one of those that is an "old head" or thinks in a way that is opposed to change, but I've seen how rare it is for people to simply respect one another. It starts at the top and works its way down. Recently I watched a clip of the current president giving a "State of The Union" address to other leaders and he wasn't able to get out a word. He was screamed at and called a liar while he was trying to give a speech. This wasn't done by random people who were in the crowd; in fact, it was done by other elected officials. The same people that were doing this would probably be the ones who would call someone a thug for disagreeing publicly with a judge in the courtroom or with a police officer in a debate. When I saw this clip, I immediately started to think about the children of these elected officials. Someone who is an elected official should be shown respect, whether you agree with everything they say or not. I wonder if the leaders who were heckling were the same ones who, as children, were talking back or shouting at teachers in the classroom? I don't know, but what I do know is that this is a common theme that has gone on since 2016 and beyond. I remember when the late much-respected war hero, Senator

John McCain was running for president. He was put on the spot by a woman who mentioned that she felt scared of an Obama presidency and that he was an "Arab." To the surprise of some, he said, "No ma'am, he's a decent family man and citizen, that I just happen to have disagreements with on fundamental issues, and that's what this campaign is all about." To the surprise of many he defended his opponent. He didn't say that he agreed with him, but he chose not to demonize someone with a different viewpoint. Years later, former President Barack Obama spoke at John McCain's funeral and shared beautiful words about the hero he was in American history. In the speech he shared that John McCain knew the importance of, "seeing past differences in search for common ground." There we had two men who might not have liked each other's policies but respected each other as men. Today things are different. Debates have become shouting matches filled with belittling each other. Unfortunately, that behavior is growing like wildfire among our young people. There's nothing wrong with debate; they're actually healthy, but disrespect is at an all-time high and our children are seeing it–and mimicking it. We have forgotten the power of our words. We've all heard the saying, "Sticks and stones may break my bones, but words will never hurt." What this quote fails to mention is that words indeed don't hurt on the outside, but they can be piercing to the soul. Let us approach this book and our lives with the respect that was shown by two American heroes of late, John McCain and former president Barack Obama.

Realizing the power we have in reshaping our perspectives for a more positive and productive outlook and life experience is one of the most valuable lessons of adulthood and the key to building an abundant community. The debate of nature versus nurture has gone on for centuries, but in my opinion, nurture will always take the cake in how important it is. Now I know that some may be thinking, well yeah environment makes sense, but it doesn't matter how much you train to be a basketball player, you've got a lot lesser chance to be an NBA star at

5'2" than someone does at 7'2", but when it comes to the core of who we are, nurturing one's beliefs, perspectives, and morals emanates from those around us.

I believe that all of us think the way that we do because we were either taught to think that way, or we experienced something that shapes our thinking. It seems easy enough, but we often forget that it's either what we are taught or what we experience that shapes us to think the way that we do. An example is my father, Christopher Robin Singleton, or "Big Chris." Big Chris was a huge Cowboys fan once he became an adult from the experience of watching amazing players like Deion Sanders and many more during his adulthood which led him to have the tradition of watching Cowboys games on Sundays. Fast forward a decade or so: I was born and I remember growing up and watching Cowboys games and cheering for them alongside my father when they won. We'd watch the games on Sunday afternoons and every now and then I could stay up late past my bedtime and watch the Cowboys game when they played on Monday Night Football. My father even bought me a small Cowboys pillow football that I'd throw with him and play catch around the house. Do you see why there would be no confusion as to why I grew up a Cowboys fan? I did so because my father taught me to be that way. The same thing with the Lakers, Syracuse Men's Basketball, R&B music, and Christmas time. I was taught by my mother and father to love these things. We are all taught things at home and although the lessons may be very different, we were all still taught, nonetheless.

Learning through experiences is different than just being taught it from someone. Experiences actually change our level of thinking. Sometimes we are taught things our whole lives and we can suddenly have one experience that changes our thinking on that specific topic forever. This happens frequently in our modern world. Whether it's politics, religion, specific diets, or even the way you view the country that you live in. When we experience something different, it often changes our thinking about the way we've been taught. What we must remember is that everyone has a story behind their stance. Everyone's thinking is likely the way it is because of what they've been taught or what they experienced. Over the next twelve chapters I'll be presenting topics that most would find extremely polarizing and presenting the stories behind the stances on both sides of the issue. You will see that whether you agree or disagree with the statements, there's always reasoning behind them. One thing I do not have any tolerance for is hate. Hate being taught and fueled in our world leads to death and destruction. That is one stance that we should all be working towards eliminating.

STANCE #1: GUNS VS. NO GUNS

Murder, self-defense, fear, and safety. There are many words that come to mind when someone hears the word "gun." Some think protection and others feel threatened. While we look at the dueling perspective of guns vs. no guns, it's important to realize that in the United States, the Constitution was written with the right to bear arms. Many historians agree that the primary reason for passing the Second Amendment was to prevent the need for the United States to have a professional standing army. In 1791 during the time it was passed, it seems it was not intended to grant a right for private individuals to keep weapons for self-defense, but to have that professional standing army at the ready. That has changed over time and many people now have weapons for self-defense to protect themselves and their families. Laws have evolved over time and in more than half the states in our country, a concealed weapons permit is needed for the carrying of firearms. These guns are registered to the name and address of the owner. Before someone can legally carry a gun here, they must go through safety training and conduct classes. Unfortunately, that doesn't keep guns out of the hands of criminals or rebellious adolescents motivated by hate. It also doesn't keep guns out of the hands of people engaging in criminal activity illegally who get their weapons illegally.

Chris's Story:

Let's start off with two stances considering the many tragic and devastating events in recent history surrounding the topic of gun control. We're setting the scene with the perspective of Chris, whose dream was to make it to Major League Baseball (MLB) and take care of his mother in her older age in the same way that she took care of him in his adolescence. His mom was a hard-working woman who smiled, put her head down, and got the job done without making any excuses, though Chris knew she never had it easy. His mother sacrificed everything for his protection and well-being.

Both he and his mom knew that the dream of playing major league baseball was a distinct possibility in Chris's future. He was only in the seventh grade when he made it onto the local high school's Junior Varsity baseball team. That is no small feat for a twelve-year-old. He was chosen among students in grade levels far above his own and playing with kids nearly four years his senior.

Together, he and his mother kept a notebook of goals that would lead to the major league level. From that 7th grade year on the JV team, Chris drove his passion all the way to college and had a spectacular college freshman season. Later that year, he was informed that his dream would be a reality in a few years because of his play. What a feeling! Chris was thrilled to be able to give his mother a sense of accomplishment for the both of them and to finally repay her for all of the investments she made in baseball gear, travel ball, baseball bats, and the countless hours she gave to the ballfield.

Chris, like many other athletes, had the dream of buying his mom a house and surprising his mom with her dream car. All his dreams of repayment were cut short on the night of June 17th, 2015. Not only was Chris's mother a hard-working speech-language pathologist, but she was also a track coach and a devoted youth minister who attended Bible study on the 17th. It was on this day that a self-proclaimed, white supremacist walked into Mother Emanuel AME church with multiple magazines of bullets and opened fire. He fired over seventy rounds of bullets and took nine lives, one of them being Chris's mother. She was forty-five years young and was shot multiple times while praying at Bible study. After hearing this news, Chris was heartbroken and his family was devastated. His dream of buying her home, and allowing her to retire while she had enough energy to travel the world was cut short. Racism and gun violence took his mother away forever.

Chris's Stance:

Today Chris hates guns. He promised himself that he would never buy a gun and he'd never keep one in his home. He's a big advocate to end gun violence and oftentimes votes for political candidates that have plans to slow down the gun violence and hate crimes we've seen in America over the last ten years. When Chris thinks about a gun he thinks about memories and moments his kids won't spend with their grandmother and those thoughts break his heart. He advocates for weapons detections systems in schools and churches and doesn't believe any place is "too sacred" to not have security.

Clark's Story:

Clark grew up in a family that was as blue-collar as they come. He'd wake up early each morning and tend to the ranch that he and his family lived on. His family had a saying, "There are no holidays on the ranch, animals have to eat and so do we." Oftentimes in elementary school, he'd get up early at the crack of dawn and help his father on the farm. By the age of eight years old, Clark had held a gun many times and had gone hunting with his father and grandfather. Not too long after that, he'd killed his first buck which brought happy tears to his grandfather's eyes. He remembers that look of pride he saw in his grandfather and constantly chased that same level of acceptance from his grandpa in everything that he did, especially being an outdoorsman. Hunting and fishing were passions that he had for most of his life. He would bond with his grandfather in the cold fall mornings waiting for deer to show themselves. He also would get the most conversation out of his father when they'd smile at one another bragging about how many doves they would shoot the next time they'd go. Although Clark's parents ran this farm, they wanted their son to have a great education and after his senior year of high school, they sent him off to Clemson University where he would study at the college of agriculture.

After graduating from Clemson, he secured a job as a ranch hand for over two-thousand acres and the owner of the land allowed him to hunt and fish on it with his family. This was perfect for Clark and his father. They would go shooting together, hunting together, and share many more laughs during this time than they ever had before. Not too long after, his grandfather passed away and his father became ill. When his grandfather died, he took possession of all his guns and rifles and went hunting and shooting continuously. He believed that the guns, the animals, and hunting brought him closer to his grandfather even after his death.

Clark's Stance:

Today, Clark loves guns. When he thinks about them, he thinks of them as something that everyone should have to protect themselves, but also to use to help communicate and bond with the young men in their lives. He doesn't believe in gun reform and thinks that every teacher should have a weapon just in case something were to happen at their school. Clark loves guns because he thinks about memories and moments with his dad and grandfather.

We Know Their Stories and Stances–Now What?

Maybe you guessed it already, but Chris is me. Clark represents a friend I have who thinks totally differently from me on this particular issue. We're cordial with each other and genuinely care about each other. We talk and disagree, but the conversations aren't tough like society often tells us they have to be.

Yes, I know that over the last four years, I've heard that we need to keep having tough conversations, but I don't think that they should be tough. You see, it shouldn't be tough to talk to a friend about sharing your truth. It may not be easy to hear something you disagree with, but I don't believe it should be a tough conversation. It really is all about how you choose to look at it and present the information. If you've built up a group of diverse friendships and/or acquaintances, the conversation may be awkward but shouldn't be tough to have. One awkward, but not tough, conversation is one that I had to have with my white baseball teammate in college. We were listening to a song that uses the N-word repetitively. At first listen I thought surely my teammate wasn't using the word while singing along, but after about two more times hearing it, I knew it was time for me to cut the music. Being one of the few black baseball players on the team, I thought it was a perfect time to teach my teammates. I had to let them know that regardless if it's in a song, no one should be saying that word. There were a few back-and-forth questions until I made it perfectly clear why he shouldn't say it anymore. With twenty or so other guys in the locker room was it awkward? Yeah, sure...for about thirty seconds, but a lesson was learned and I'm still friends with that teammate to this day. I know he will never forget that conversation we had and that it permanently changed his behavior for good. It's important to point out, though, that he and the rest of the team had and still have an obligation to stand up and have those conversations with other white people if they see it happening in front of them. To sit back in silence when a white person uses the N-word is taking the side of the oppressor and prevents real and influential progress.

As we continue to have these conversations, it usually becomes a lot easier to communicate the points we are trying to make once we have had the dialogue a couple of times. It's important to remember that when you are the one giving "the talking to," you should do your best to speak to the other person without accusation, even if you are trying to change their mind. We must remember that when people feel uncomfortable in a situation, they may also feel attacked and become defensive. Preface this with something along the lines of, "I'm only telling you this because I care about you, and I know you care about me." Meet them on that human plane where we are all equal. Be gentle in your pursuit of these conversations for this reason, but don't be afraid to have them altogether because you fear someone might get mad at you. Do not be afraid to correct someone–your boss, your colleague, your grandmother, or your friend. It's all the same. Doing the work is letting them know when something's right or wrong. The only difference is how you do that. For some, it's standing up and cutting the music, for other's it's an email informing them why and how something was incorrect. Other times it's a heart-to-heart conversation when nobody's around.

Think about a time someone maybe corrected something you did or said, that you later really appreciated them for pointing it out. It's almost as if, had they kept it to themselves, they wouldn't have been doing you any favors at all.

Another (less obvious) thing I've talked to my friends about is a question I got asked the other day. This person said, "Do you think people would rather be called African American or Black?" I answered, "Man, honestly, I've never really thought about it, but for me probably Black, not African American. You honestly don't know anything about the person's culture or heritage so black would be best in my opinion. They could be so many other things while still being black. If I'm cool with them, I'd ask." I told him that it used to be insensitive or disrespectful to call someone a person of color or minority, but we are in such a blended world it's hard to assume you know anything before you start talking to someone. In that instance, I shared my truth with him. For others, it may be different, but that's what I prefer and I let him know that. Same thing when I asked a friend what keeping kosher meant for him. I Googled it, but I didn't know if he was orthodox or unorthodox when it came to his Jewish faith. When you're in conversation with your friends/peers/coworkers, the key is to listen to understand, not listen to tell someone when/where they're wrong. I lived an example of this. I've always been one to support local movements before global movements because sometimes the global movements are stained with controversy or once they go global you may not agree with everything they stand for globally. I was sitting with a gentleman who was at least seventy years old, and he kept going on about Black Lives Matter and the movement and how people were causing more harm than good. I didn't interrupt; I didn't shout. I just waited until he was done and asked him the question, "Do you believe Black Lives Matter?" His answer was, "Absolutely I do, I just don't believe in the movement." I told him I definitely understood where he was coming from, but I also wanted to get him to think about any movement. Chances are, we are not going to agree with everything that is said, but we most likely would believe in the statement.

I believe we must be intentional about celebrating other people's cultures. When they know that the questions you're asking are coming from a place of love, they'd be happy to tell you their truth. I recently had an encounter with a young woman, and I noticed she had some sort of drawing on her hand. It was a beautiful design really and I had seen them before, but I didn't know if it was a cultural thing or just something that women were doing as a trend. I asked her about it and immediately saw a huge smile, "My mom actually did this for me!" She said, "Thank you for asking. We actually just celebrated a Muslim holiday and got all dressed up and this art on my hands was the final touch to my outfit." She proceeded to tell me more about her culture, and her family and I learned a lot. You see I didn't need to say the right thing... it wasn't uncomfortable for me, and I learned something new and I'm sure she felt like she was in a very inclusive safe space around me.

Throughout history in the United States and around the world, there's always been a certain level of tolerance instead of genuine love for those who are not like us. I believe we need to start at home with those that we love and confront them in a loving way even when the topic makes us have butterflies in our stomachs.

This courage was shown in a story that I heard from an attendee at a conference where I was speaking. She approached me and applauded me for the courage that I showed in sharing this message of unity and love in rural Alabama where I was. She then proceeded to tell me it took courage for her to have a conversation with her father about the athletes he had on his football team. She told me that he was a head football coach for the local high school she went to in the 1980s. She said that their football team was very diverse and their school reflected that as well. She then mentioned that her dad would have a large cookout for the team once a year at their home, and at the cookout, they'd always have everyone outside. She noticed that he would never let his black players inside their home. She didn't think much of it until one cookout she saw him let one of the white players use their restroom, but asked the black player to just go out back by the trees outside. The rest of the day her stomach hurt and she knew she had to say something. She talked to her mom and dad about it that night and basically told him, if he can have black players on his team, they need to be able to trust him, and making someone go to the restroom outside because they're black was flat out wrong. Her mom and dad agreed with her after that night because she was so upfront and vocal with her dad about how she felt. From that point forward, he never had that rule anymore. I had heard of similar stories but hadn't heard something like this from a coach and I especially didn't think this would be happening in the 1980s, but I learned that this was the case. Her courage to be open with her family led to change happening. The conversation wasn't hard for her; she just needed to have enough courage to make it happen.

STANCE #2: OPEN IMMIGRATION VS. BORDER CONTROL

As Americans, we often hear conversations relating to our country serving as a refuge for those in countries where war and poverty trump healthcare and education. There tends to be an increase in these discussions when other countries are in peril. The most common arguments against immigration involve jobs, wages, and the existing poverty level and resources in America.

The topic of immigration cannot be considered without also considering the subject of our borders and border policies. Some Americans believe the impact of immigration on their personal lives is minimal. Many on the opposing side of immigration and border control reform operate with the notion that immigrants will take American jobs, negatively impact overall industry wage, cause an uptick in crime, and absorb federal and state resources allotted to our own citizens living in oppressive or impoverished conditions.

Others who want to bring family members and friends into the United States believe that everyone deserves a chance at the American Dream. They believe that this country is the best place for someone to start with nothing and work their way up to a better life that may not have been given to them in their homeland.

Juanita's Story

Juanita was only ten years old when her family made the dangerous trip from Honduras to the United States. Her mother was a single mom and had been in a toxic relationship and wanted to break free from her abuser. Her mother's plan was to run away to the United States where her family would have a safe place to sleep at night. They set out on their journey and had to stop in Mexico before meeting with the group that was going to see them through to the United States. After living in Mexico for about three months, they finally mustered up enough courage to take on the treacherous journey. Juanita remembers being scared and looking to her mom to see if she, too, shared that same fear, but her mom was so determined to get them to the U. S. that she showed no fear and looked almost as if she welcomed any challenge sent her way.

Things were going well until they got to the Rio Grande River. Juanita and her mom were with three others on a small inflatable boat at midnight trying to cross the river. Without headlights, flashlights, or anything to help them see, Juanita remembers the water's current being a lot faster than anyone had thought it would be. Eventually something in the water overturned their inflatable boat. When that happened, everyone in the boat flipped out and scurried to try to climb back on. At ten years old Juanita was the second youngest on the boat, only older than a three-year-old boy who had been thrown outside of the boat, too. Thankfully she and the three-year-old wore life jackets but in the heat of the moment, her mom was left off the boat. She remembers crying and yelling for her mom to swim back to the boat, but the water had picked up speed and they couldn't catch up with her mom. Juanita then realized that her mom wasn't going to be able to complete the trip with them. She saw her mom blow her a kiss and continue to try to fight, but she wasn't strong enough to keep herself from being taken by the current. She screamed that she loved Juanita and that was the last thing she ever heard from her mom.

Hours later, after crossing, border patrol came and got Juanita and everyone else that was traveling in that small boat. They took Juanita to a holding facility for all illegal immigrants who were either caught or turned themselves in to border patrol and she stayed there for a month before going into foster care. Juanita promised herself she would create that beautiful life for herself that her mom dreamt of and she eventually graduated college, got a great job, and became a U. S. citizen. Although she believed she achieved the American dream, years of foster care and losing her mom always lingered in her mind. As a child she often asked the question, "Why couldn't we just drive to the United States and make it here safe instead of putting our lives in so much danger?"

Juanita's Stance

Juanita believes that everyone who wants to enter the U. S. should be able to do so without putting their lives in danger. She believes that America should have an easy process for people traveling near and far to enter, without having to cross over things like the Rio Grande. She also believes that across the border there should be better facilities for those who are living in holding homes temporarily before being granted asylum. She disagrees with those who wish to make it more difficult for immigrants to enter the United States.

Brandon's Story

Brandon grew up in Dallas, Texas, to two very hard-working parents. Growing up, there were plenty of times when his parents left for work when it was dark and came home when it was dark, leaving him at home to fend for himself and figure out what he could make for dinner. Both mom and dad prided themselves on honesty and doing things the right way. It didn't take long for Brandon to want to go out and work to help out with bills around the house. If you worked with him, you could easily see the work ethic that he displayed–just like his parents. By age thirteen he would help his dad out on construction sites after school and on the weekends. It started off with him hauling off old junk or excess materials from the homes that were being renovated while the older men and women were working on putting walls and electrical components together.

Over time, the crews that Brandon's dad was on started to teach him each trade that they were experts in. He would spend a day or two with the handymen that were working on the plumbing and HVAC, learn a little bit, then the next few days he would transition to drywall and painting. Brandon would do this so much that by the time he was eighteen he knew just about all the skills and responsibilities required to build a house. Oftentimes he would ask his father why the crew wouldn't all put their money together and build a home of their own. His father would reply that the crew needed the money they made for bills and that afterward the little money they did have, they all must save for their kids to go to college.

Brandon set out to make a change with this cycle so that he would be able to get his guys paid more and be able to make a large profit after selling the property. At eighteen years of age, he decided to forego college and, instead, started his own real estate company. Initially doing small jobs here and there, over time he started getting bids from large home builders to build homes from start to finish. By the age of twenty-five Brandon was getting bids for him to build homes from people all over the country that were moving to Dallas. He was paying his father and the former employees more than anyone else in the Dallas area and felt so much pride in his business. This was the case until a new company came in underbidding all the other contractors in the area. The company consisted of a Latin American owner, Luis, who employed only illegal immigrants. At first, Brandon figured that he'd be OK, but over time every bid would go to Luis and his crew. Eventually, Brandon had to lay off the people that he had trained under and it broke his heart. He knew he couldn't afford to charge rates as low as Luis and slowly but surely his once-successful business became a struggling small business and eventually he lost it all.

Brandon's Stance

Brandon feels as though our country has failed us due to the number of illegal immigrants we allow into this country. Brandon believes that there should be a more strenuous green card process and that we already have enough people in this country who weren't born here and adding more takes jobs away from hard-working Americans. He believes immigrants impact local small businesses in a negative way. When voting, the only thing that he looks at in potential political candidates is the policies they have related to border protection/patrol. Brandon wasn't raised to dislike Hispanics, but it is clear that he is now prejudiced toward those who have Spanish accents when speaking English.

Many people who agree with Brandon would say that there are ways that people can enter the country legally without putting themselves or their families in danger. In some cases, immigrants have the time and resources to do so. Take Julie, for example, an immigrant from Mexico who is also a legal citizen of the United States of America. She recalls her experience coming through customs and border patrol and how it was her first taste of what her life in America was going to be like. Her father, Manuel, was a street food vendor and her mother stayed at home tending to her two brothers and sisters, one of whom has special needs. It was difficult for Manuel to make ends meet with bills and the lack of access to proper healthcare for their specific needs. Though her family went through all the proper processes and paperwork for immigration, they are still met to this day with judgment and doubt as it relates to their citizenship and validity as contributing members of society. America offered a place where she and her family could continue to work without fear of being taken advantage of and they would have access to proper healthcare and higher education.

We Know Their Stories and Stances–Now What?

We know their stories and there's empathy for Brandon losing his business and having to fire the very men and women that trained him as a kid. We also know how hard it must have been for Juanita losing a loved one just to get a shot at a better life. They don't have to agree, but both should know that there's a story behind both of their stances. In a world of understanding, Brandon may have to recognize that losing business to someone who charges less and does the same quality or better work is just the cost of doing business. It happens every day with technology creating software for robots to replace a lot of factory workers and it's going to keep happening in the future. Juanita may have to recognize that unlimited immigration can have negative consequences for America and its citizens.

The key is to be ahead of the curve in any and every industry or make your work so good that you will be the person people go to no matter the price. Juanita may need to recognize that letting everyone in without order may lead to more chaos than good and it definitely makes it hard for those that come here legally. As sad as it may be, her mom knew that not completing the trip was a possibility so taking it out on the American government unfortunately won't bring her back.

Face Your Fears

Common ground is found when we realize that we're all afraid of something. Juanita is afraid that lives will be lost, just like her mom lost her life. Brandon is afraid that more businesses will be shut down, and Julie is afraid that she will never be accepted as an American. We fear what we don't know, so learning about the opposing side's point of view helps to eliminate that fear.

Let's talk about fear. What are your fears? Why do you fear these things? Are there some things you used to fear that you no longer do? What are they? How did you overcome that fear? Do you believe that fear was valid now that you are no longer afraid?

Fear controls our thoughts and behaviors as much as our hopes and dreams do. What we fear is what we believe can harm us and our well-being. Though a person's fear can saturate uncertainty when we create space for curiosity and seek understanding, sharing our fears will help us be open and live a life of vulnerability.

If our goal is to truly live in peaceful harmony with those around us, regardless of their lifestyles or beliefs, then vulnerability is naturally our next focus. In *Daring Greatly* by Brene Brown, she describes this idea of vulnerability as The Three C's: Courage, Compassion, and Connection (Brown, 2012).

We must have the courage to be honest with ourselves and others in conversations that include people who have divergent opinions. We need to remember to have compassion for others, and especially ourselves, as we become able to extend grace which leads to understanding and a willingness to connect with those who are not like us despite our differences.

STANCE #3:
BLACK LIVES MATTER VS. ALL LIVES MATTER

The Black Lives Matter (BLM) movement began with the hashtag, #BlackLivesMatter after the acquittal of police officers involved in the shooting deaths of innocent young black men. BLM continued to establish itself as a worldwide movement after the deaths of many other men like them. This movement protests police brutality and systemic racism that particularly impacts the Black community in America. Throughout the rest of this chapter, I want you to think about the words, *Black Lives Matter* as a movement and not just as an organization.

CHAINSAWSUIT.COM

Kris Straub/Chainsawsuit

Photo: Kris Straub

I'm sure we've all seen that graphic that circulated on the internet (above) during the BLM Movement. Two houses sit side-by-side but one is on fire and the other is not. A man stands in front of the house that is not on fire with a hose shouting, "All Lives Matter!" But it's not All Lives whose house is on fire. Using that term to challenge BLM is the same as letting a house burn down because we were using the hose to water the grass. It's not uncommon for people to be focused solely on themselves in times when movements such as BLM are in the news. We've seen it happen during the civil rights movement and other times when people feel attacked. Before they help someone else, they want to make sure they don't lose their own status. Putting out the fire on whatever house is burning is progress, regardless of what demographic with which you identify.

Andrew's Story

One evening when a young Black man named Andrew was going for a jog in his neighborhood, two trucks of white men assumed he was up to no good and chased him down trying to block his running path. Andrew was scared for his life, as these men seemed to be intent on imposing force and violence upon him. For what? He wasn't sure. Andrew was just going for his nightly run when he was suddenly ganged up on by a group of older white men who clearly were racially motivated by hate. In an attempt to defend himself, he tried reasoning with the men, asking them what they wanted from him and why they were so certain he was a criminal. Without thinking, another white man pulled a shotgun from his truck and shot Andrew on the spot with no cause or self-defensive actions–which the shooter later tried to plead was the case. All three men involved were charged with numerous counts of hate crime and murder. They will now live the rest of their lives in prison known as the white men who killed an innocent black man when he was going for his nightly run because of their racial prejudice against black people in America.

Andrew's Family's Stance

Andrew's family believes as black individuals in America, oppression and prejudice run through the very veins that bind this country. The Constitution, for example, is considered a living and breathing document that stands for all humanity, except for when it was first written to leave out black men and women who were not property owners. They believe the institution of racism in America goes beyond our history books where we learned of the abolition of slavery and Jim Crow laws. As time progresses, it seems to them that racial injustices only change their form. In the present day, they believe that Black Americans are feared solely because of the color of their skin, often as a result of how they have been portrayed in the media and on crime television shows. They believe there is no reason for racially motivated crimes at any point in history, much less today. As people who aren't threatened by society's racial inclinations, they must stand with those who are being targeted and serve as a voice among the nations. They believe that many white people don't value the lives of black people in America. They believe if you see a person of color being questioned or treated with any sort of injustice, you have a duty as a fellow citizen to protect them and speak up if you see someone trying to instigate a negative situation. They march, protest, and have signs everywhere reminding people that Black Lives Matter.

Jerry's Story

Jerry grew up in a town without any racial diversity in West Virginia, where the poorest of the poor and richest of the rich were all white. He grew up in a trailer park and came from uneducated parents who were unable to take him anywhere to expand his perspective of the world. Jerry eventually became a successful stockbroker and moved from the middle of nowhere West Virginia to succeeding in an industry and a location in which he has no familiarity with anyone. The first week he moved to New York City, his bike was stolen by two young black kids. This was the first time he'd ever been a victim of a crime like this.

Jerry doesn't understand the concept of Black Lives Matter. He thinks that all lives matter, and he has never done anything bad to someone who is black but he has robbed and nobody said that white lives matter. Saying black lives matter to him doesn't make sense because it makes him feel like the struggling poor in his hometown don't matter. As someone who made it a point to move out of the town and make a name for himself from nothing, he feels like All Lives Matter is an appropriate response to the recent news of Black Lives Matter. He believes that every person should have the right to be protected and we should be fighting for the rights of all people, not just black people.

Jerry's Stance

Amidst his success as an adult, Jerry always carried prejudice against black men because he recalls how he was robbed during his first week in New York. It's hard for him to picture a black man without thinking of the time he was a victim of this crime. That single instance shaped his view of Black Americans as a whole and prevented him from ever engaging in productive conversations or establishing beneficial relationships with any people of color. He feels like the issue of the oppressed and the righteous goes beyond skin color and that the people back in his hometown are still struggling, even though they are white. His stance is that he's from a trailer park, came from nothing, and worked his behind off to make a better life for himself. He asks himself, "Does my life not matter? What about the little poor white kids back home in West Virginia?"

We Know Their Stories and Stances–Now What?

No matter where we are on our journey of supporting the fact Black Lives Matter or if you're still growing and need time to heal from what you've been through, we need to know that these conversations happen everywhere. Diversity, Equity, Inclusion, and Belonging (DEIB) are something that was long overdue in many organizations and are finally coming to the forefront of organizations helping them grow in areas they've never even scratched the surface of previously. Even though many are learning about their biases and making progress, frequently people still ask the question, "What exactly is DEIB?" If that's you then here's a definition of each of them for you.

Diversity-The state of being diverse means the practice or quality of including/involving people from a wide range of socioeconomic, cultural, racial, and ethnic backgrounds and of all gender identities and sexual orientations.

Equity- The quality of being fair and impartial.

Inclusion- Presenting an equal opportunity to each and every individual no matter their independent obstacles, including access to education and resources.

Belonging- Belonging is a sense of fitting in or feeling like you are an important member of a group.

Oftentimes when we hear about **DEIB**, we become overwhelmed and don't know where to start. For me, I try to explain these terms in the simplest of forms: I believe that diversity is a number, equity is fairness, inclusion is involvement and belonging is making someone feel like they matter to you. It includes:

- Representing all kinds of kinds from all walks of life.
- The welcoming of any and all personal characteristic traits.
- The coexistence of variable lifestyles, personal truths, and religious belief systems which are essential to humanity.

Why does diversity matter? Inherent bias is rooted in a lack of understanding about others. These are the very forms of bias that amplify racial and gender stereotypes which ultimately affect how people see those around them with whom they associate. Diversity challenges the idea that something different must be bad. Just because you might be unfamiliar with something, its difference doesn't equate to inferiority. Unfortunately, this is how many people with prejudiced views ended up thinking the way that they do. We are healing generations of trauma by creating diverse workplaces and community environments where everyone is not only included, but also feels a sense of belonging among others.

There are four core elements of diversity are *internal, external, organizational,* and *worldview* (Alliant International University, 2020). **Internal diversity** refers to any characteristic or trait that a person is born with. This includes one's sex, race, ethnicity, gender, sexual orientation, nationality, or physical ability. **External diversity** covers any attribute, experience, or circumstance that defines someone's sense of self and identity. This includes socioeconomic status, education level, marital status, religion, and physical location. **Organizational diversity** relates to a collective group of colleagues with various job functions, varied levels of work experience, seniority, and management are all considered. **Worldview diversity** includes a broad range of beliefs, political associations, culture, and travel experiences. Basically, anything and everything could possibly influence the way we interpret and view the world.

We can't talk about diversity and inclusion without also discussing the topics of equity and equality. While the terms equity and equality may sound similar, the implementation of one versus the other can lead to dramatically different outcomes for marginalized people. **Equality** means each individual or group of people is given the same resources or opportunities.

Equity recognizes that each person has different circumstances and allocates the exact resources and opportunities needed to reach an equal outcome. I always say diversity is a number, equity is what's fair, inclusion is a universal feeling and belonging is humanity. All these things are essential for our unity.

So how are we supposed to solve this problem? After knowing these things, I believe that selflessness can help us move forward. For Jerry, it always came back to the question, "What about me?" or "What about the kids back home where I'm from?" This mentality makes it seem as though because it's not about you, then it doesn't matter. Selflessness can help create change. When something happens in the world, it may not be about you, but you can still go to the aid of whoever is hurting at the time. When people with greater or more resources are able to come together to provide what they have in excess to meet the needs of people who are missing opportunities that would better their lives, this is where progress is made. Here's an example:

Equality is every single kid getting a Chromebook or some sort of laptop for their schoolwork during the COVID-19 pandemic. Equality is assigning all students the same homework and assignments based on the same curriculum and school standards. The challenge of equity is now introduced to those students who don't have consistent access to wifi. The kids who didn't have wifi at home would be automatically marked as absent for not logging into their classroom portal. They missed assignments and fell behind in their lessons because of this. You might say, Chris, it's easy to go to Starbucks or McDonald's or the library but what about the kid who has a single parent and a one-car household? When their only form of transportation is unavailable because of their parents' jobs, they're probably not making that trip and who can blame them? We can't expect kids to willingly bike miles and miles to the nearest free Wi-Fi connection. We can't assume that each student goes home to the same kind of setup and family dynamic.

Equity is when businesses donate Wi-Fi routers to underserved communities for those students. The COVID-19 pandemic uncovered a lot of different things that kids who are less fortunate than others were struggling with, one of them being Wi-Fi access. Equity was accomplished when companies like T-Mobile stepped up and gave students the opportunity for success and said, in effect, "Let us be a part of the change for these students" and called it Project 10 Million (T-Mobile, 2022). Project 10 Million is an initiative aimed at delivering internet connectivity to millions of underserved student households at no cost. Partnering with school districts across the country, the program offers free high-speed data and free mobile hotspots—and access to at-cost laptops and tablets. This is equity because not every child needs this, but the ones who do will have an even playing field to be able to accomplish their school tasks and have the opportunity for success in their studies.

Photo Credit: The Second Line Education Blog

This is a popular graphic that I think illustrates the concept of equity versus equality quite well. In the image, we see three people at various heights standing behind the fence, trying to look over. On one side, only the tall kids can see over the fence despite them all being given a box to stand on. Some would consider that equality since all of them were given the same thing. It just so happens that the taller kids got the view because of genetics. Now, equity in this situation looks a lot different. Equity is setting each kid up with the thing that makes them as tall as they need to be they can all see with ease.

STANCE #4:
POLICE REFORM VS. BACK THE BLUE

Many Americans in recent years have been calling for police reform. It seems as though there have been so many lives lost at the hands of police officer misconduct. Many would argue that this has always happened in our history, but now it is coming to the attention of the masses because of the power of police body cameras and people recording such events to post on social media. Police reform means training officers and other law enforcement personnel to consider the ways these senseless deaths could have been avoided had they acted in a manner of professionalism and safety for all parties involved. It also means moving funds from police departments and giving them to community-backed organizations that could help with mental health or youth programs to prevent crime from happening in the future.

The *Back the Blue* movement was created by Attorney General Ashley Moody as a countermovement to police protests that highlight law enforcement officers, citizens, and organizations taking extraordinary steps to forging positive relationships between law enforcement and the communities they serve (Moody, 2022). This movement was to show support and acknowledge that there are many good officers who are being harassed for simply trying to protect the people and places that they are hired to serve.

Michelle's Story

Michelle's son, Mikey, was a big-time athlete who had offers from colleges all across the country. He was on the debate team and his dream was to become a lawyer once he finished competing as a runner for his future university and for the United States Olympics team. Six months before Mikey's big signing day, he was killed on his way home from track practice. He was driving home and was pulled over by the police because his license plate had expired one month earlier. Mikey had a rough relationship with police officers and didn't trust them entirely because he saw his father get arrested as a kid and cried for hours knowing that his dad might not come back home. Because of this experience, he never wanted to be alone with officers when being pulled over so he drove almost two miles further with the police behind him so he could pull over into a gas station where there was light and, potentially, other people.

After arriving there, the officers were upset that Mikey didn't pull over when they put their lights on and were aggressive with Mikey. Mikey didn't like the tone they were using and told them they needed to get the officer above them to come because he didn't feel safe and didn't want to cooperate until their superior was there. They never called for backup and insisted that Mikey give them his license and registration. Without saying a word, upset that they wouldn't adhere to his request, Mikey reached for the glove compartment where his registration was. When doing that one of the officers saw a weapon in the glove compartment. After Mikey grabbed the registration and turned toward the officers, it was too late. One of the officers had already shot Mikey two times in his shoulder, killing him almost instantly. Michelle always kept a taser gun in the car that she used just for protection for her family and had recently used Mikey's car while hers was in the shop. Mikey knew nothing about the taser and didn't reach for it as it was noted that he had the registration, not the taser, in his hand when he was killed. The officers responsible were found not guilty in accordance with the evidence presented and it was ruled as a sad and tragic accident. Michelle's son's killers served no time in prison after being dismissed from the police force during the investigation.

Michelle can't help but feel like her son was murdered and officers should have known that Mikey–with no previous history of any crimes–wasn't a kid that would be trying to hurt them. She believes their training was flawed and they gave Mikey no warning or anything before they killed him. The taser was behind the registration and proper training would have let them know that they were in no danger; it was only a kid who was scared and nervous. Instead, her innocent child was seen as a threat to the law enforcement officers who passed him on his way home that night. She believes if her son was white, he'd still be here.

Michelle's Stance

Michelle believes strongly in police reform because she feels that there is not enough accountability in the current processes of law enforcement. She feels as though the ways the Black community is targeted heavily by police is a direct result of the Reagan administration's War on Drugs decades ago. She feels as though this was America's way of targeting Black communities, particularly Black men. She and her son in no way have ever felt safe around a police officer; in fact, she feels a sense of overwhelming anxiety and anger toward them because her son's life was so unfairly and carelessly taken. To her, the police don't actually protect her from anything. Michelle hopes to see measures taken by the government at the local, state, and federal levels to investigate police misconduct and corruption.

Jamal's Story

Jamal is twelve years old and from Charlotte, North Carolina. He's a good student, but his main passions are drawing and he loves listening to music. Jamal says he has a great life, but many look at Jamal's circumstances and say that he's got obstacles lined up against him. When looking from the outside, it's easy to see that his life hasn't been easy. For most of his life he's had to take care of his three younger siblings, tucking them in bed and feeding them the dinner their mom left out before she heads to her second job. His mom works so hard doing multiple jobs to be sure that her kids don't want for anything. Jamal is a sophisticated young man and takes pride in the fact that he taught his little brothers and sister how to tie their shoes before they got to kindergarten. Jamal believes that his biggest dream in life is to buy his mom their first house to repay her for working so hard for him and his siblings and be able to draw photos for animated television shows.

As Jamal has grown up, he's always known who the police were and was told to stay away from them and not say much to them. He was told that by his family members because that was always the rule that they had on their street. That has been easy for Jamal to do because he's always had a hatred for the police since he saw his dad get beat and arrested in front of their house four years ago. Jamal and his dad were playing basketball at the local park just like they always did. On their way home, his father was approached by officers and asked tons of questions that he didn't want to answer. Jamal's dad got frustrated and Jamal vividly remembers that next, he saw his father being wrestled to the ground by four officers. He remembers seeing the officers strike his father and scream at him for resisting arrest, but Jamal felt like he wasn't resisting arrest at all. He thought his dad was only trying to cover up his face so he wouldn't be hurt any further. After seeing this firsthand, Jamal had an extremely rough patch in school. He skipped school frequently and on the days that he did go to school, he struggled with his conduct and would get into altercations with other kids from his school. At court for his father, he begged and pleaded for his dad to come home, but to him, those cries weren't heard and nobody cared enough to do anything to help ease his pain. He went four years without playing his favorite sport because it was something that he believed only he and his father could do together.

Jamal's Stance

Jamal doesn't like the police. He feels that they take away fathers, husbands, and influential men in the world. He believes he could never have respect or be cool with anyone as an officer.

It's easy to see why Jamal doesn't like officers; he has preconceived notions about who they are and what they do. He feels this way because in his eyes he sees that officers took away his father for four years of his life. He also believes that these officers made him grow up early and take care of his younger siblings because he had to help out while his mom worked multiple jobs. My hope is that Jamal can understand that there are good officers in the world that signed up for the job to serve and protect and that not every one of them wants to hurt people.

Sadie's Story

One of the things Sadie has always wanted to do in her life was to become a loving mother to her children and loving wife to her husband. Sadie grew up in a household that didn't value marriage and she felt that she was neglected. She recalls times in her life when she needed help but didn't feel like asking her mom or her dad, so she just did things on her own. At the age of twenty-one she found the love of her life in a police officer by the name of Brady. After meeting Brady, her gift and her dream came to fruition as she married him and they had their first child. After four years of a blissful marriage, Sadie recalls getting a call on her cell phone about something that happened while Brady was working. She learned that her husband Brady just saved someone's life by jumping off a building. She was told that a man was going to jump and her husband leapt off of the edge and grabbed him, keeping his feet on the ground.

She was ecstatic that he was OK, but fearful that she almost lost her husband and the father to their child. She's so grateful that her husband has a job in which he saves lives, but she's nervous every day that it may be the last day he leaves their house. Selfishly, she doesn't ever want to see him put his life in danger for someone who wants to take their life or has no regard for the officer's life. She prides herself that her husband took the oath to serve their city and protect the men and women that live there, but she hates the fact that he has to put his life on the line daily for those that may not have any regard for his own life. She made a vow to him that they would be together until death does them apart, she just doesn't want that to come as a result of him getting killed by protecting others that wouldn't do the same for him.

Sadie's Stance

Sadie's stance is that she "backs the blue" and can't agree with anyone who believes in police reform that would hinder the work of police officers. She thinks that officers are overworked, and underpaid and criminals–regardless of their age–should be punished for any and every crime that they commit.

We Know Their Stories and Stances–Now What?

The way that both Sadie and Jamal can be united is by hearing each other's story. As a family woman, I'm sure that Sadie would understand the pain that Jamal feels by not having his father and uncle there to lead him in life. She won't agree with the blame that he places on officers, but there will be empathy there when she realizes that it is coming from not having love. The same way that her child could grow up hating the person that jumped off the roof had her dad been hurt when he saved him, is the same way that Jamal is feeling for the officers that took his family away from him. As for Jamal, I wholeheartedly believe in community policing. The School Resource Officer or someone from Jamal's school should break down the fact that they don't want Jamal to be without a father, they simply want to make sure that their community is safe and when you break the law there are consequences. Easier said than done, I know, but I've seen it happen. I've seen kids go from not wanting anything to do with police officers, to falling in love with officers after consistent care and unconditional love. My friend, Officer Bloom, in Fargo North Dakota, is a perfect example. I'll never forget going to speak to thousands of students with him and hearing him rap about hope and joy to all the students. Here was a white man in a police uniform. He broke barriers and made relationships with students that I know for a fact walked into the auditorium with a sour taste in their mouths about police officers. When they left, their hearts and minds were changed. In FULL UNIFORM he would rap and play basketball with the kids in school. The gyms would erupt in applause afterward because the kids finally saw him as someone they could relate to and quite frankly, it was dope to see a young white cop change generations of perspectives for people in a matter of two minutes in a packed gymnasium!

For most that back the blue, it's triggering when people say, "defund the police," but in many cases they aren't saying they want less officers; in fact, people are pleading for more community policing. They aren't saying, "abolish the police and law enforcement." Defunding means reallocating funds throughout local government to places like mental health services and other areas that would better serve the people in these communities with saturated police patrols. There are so many different things that people who "back the blue" as well as those who want to "defund the police" can do to make our streets and our world safer. At the end of the day, we all want to feel safe and know that our kids are safe at school, at home, or on the way home from track practice.

STANCE #5: PRISON REFORM VS. MASS INCARCERATION

Criminal justice and prison reform as it relates to mass incarceration is a human rights movement that works to attempt to improve conditions inside prisons, improve the effectiveness of the judicial system, and implement alternatives to incarceration. It also ensures the reinstatement of those whose lives are impacted by crimes.

The term mass incarceration refers to the way our society and the legal system respond to crimes, especially if it relates to sentences involving non-violent drug offenses.

Chelsey's Story

Chelsey grew up in Atlanta, Georgia, where her father spent most of his time in and out of prison for nonviolent, drug-related crimes. She watched her father struggle to assimilate back into society each time he would be released from jail and was deeply bothered by the fact that each time he went in, he came out with no additional resources or rehabilitation to help him stay out once he reached the end of his sentence. She felt as though the prison system let him down by not preparing him for life outside of prison. Each time he left, it was almost as if they expected to see him right back there just a few months later.

Prison reform, to her, means working with inmates–both men and women–toward a future outside of prison. Part of this includes education and therapy for those incarcerated to help equip them with the necessary tools to enter back into society with success. Success for those recently released from prison is simple: not going back to prison.

She works with her local legislatures to improve prison conditions by lobbying for additional resources and donations to help inmates transition back into society once they are released with skills and coping mechanisms to help better themselves for the long term. She works towards collective action from the local level to effect change on a regional and national level in America.

Chelsey's Stance

Chelsea believes that our prison system is set up to bring people back to prison once they leave. She believes that too many people are away from their families for years and years for offenses which merited a much more lenient punishment. She pleads with government officials and prisons to put more effort towards teaching and helping those who are currently incarcerated so they can be productive members of society when they are released. She sees a lot of prison programming that only focuses on keeping the inmates busy instead of bettering themselves for a future outside of prison. Without proper education and resources, she asks, how can we expect those who have been in jail for most of their lives to re-enter society easily? We must work with those who are incarcerated toward a future free of crime and punishment. At the end of the day, prisoners are people, some of whom have done things that are legal today, but they were incarcerated for it many years ago. Her stance is that parole shouldn't be possible only in 10, 20, or even 30 years or more; instead, once someone turns their life around for the better and becomes a model citizen, they shouldn't be treated like a criminal for the rest of their lives.

Larry's Story

Larry is a retired public defender for the city of Atlanta, Georgia. He spent his career representing convicts who could not afford to retain their own lawyer for defense on trial. He recalls one inmate who he worked with closely on his plans to reduce his sentence and how disappointed he was each time he would see him back in the courtroom after being released. He often represented the same people case after case, year after year, and wondered what would have to happen for these people to make a lasting change in behavior that wouldn't land them back in prison.

It is difficult for a defense case to hold up in court when the defendant's record is stacked with the same offenses time after time. Even nonviolent drug offenses can add up over time and send someone to prison for years. There isn't much he could do for the young men and women he kept seeing in and out of jail for the same illegal activity. He finally was able to catch a big break and he won a large case for a guy that was supposedly a robber in a crime that he insisted he never committed. After he was released from prison this same guy assaulted a family of five leaving one in the hospital for almost a month with serious injuries. Larry was heartbroken that even when he finally won a case for someone, that person went out and hurt a family in the middle of the night. It was hard for him to sleep knowing that had it not been for him, maybe none of that would have happened.

Larry's Stance

Larry now believes that when someone is charged with a crime, they need to show significant improvement while in jail or they will come out doing the same thing over and over again. Larry thinks sentences should be shorter, but the whole sentence should be served and men and women shouldn't be allowed back on the streets with the same mentality they had when they went into prison. No matter what we do inside the prisons, if someone chooses to go back to the life that landed them in prison in the first place, that is their choice. It doesn't help their case when they've come back to court with the same charges they beat the first few times and it makes you wonder if perhaps they weren't given a long enough sentence the first time to teach them the lesson they so desperately need to learn.

We Know Their Stories and Stances–Now What?

I personally have seen how someone can permanently turn their life around for good. Unfortunately, the way our court system is set up, they can be treated like criminals for the rest of their lives regardless of how hard they work to change and how sincere they are in their efforts. Take my friend Damon, for example. Damon was sentenced to life in prison. Through diligence and commitment, he used his time behind bars to self-reflect and grow as an individual because he truly believed that there was life for him outside of his current situation. He utilized every resource he could, learning from anyone and anything he could to make sure prison did not change the man he was destined to be. He was dedicated to making productive use of his time and not "getting comfortable" in jail just because he was sentenced to serve a life term.

His perseverance and determination ultimately led him back into the courtroom to hear that his sentence had made parole. He was given a true release date, something he had been working for since day one.

Days turn into months and Damon is eventually a free man again with nothing to lose and everything to gain. He also now has a felony on his record, however. That poses a huge obstacle to his opportunities in the job market today, because many people write ex-convicts off as a lost cause or not worth the potential liability that hiring them entails. What is someone who just got out of jail supposed to do when they spend all their newfound freedom searching for a job only to find doors shut and phone calls left unreturned? For many people in this situation, push comes to shove and they get scared, which triggers the only thing they know how to do to survive. For a lot of these men who have recently been released, it means going back to selling illegal substances or getting involved in other non-violent crimes. In a lot of these cases, they are afraid that they will stay unemployed and overlooked and come up short financially. After all, there's not a lot of money to be made in prison. When you start your new life with the odds against you, it can feel like the only way out is through the very way you came in—which for a lot of men puts them right back in jail.

Now imagine a world where programs are in place to educate and mentor these people who are soon to be released back into society with connections and processes that set them up for success in a way that not only benefits themselves, but also the entire community. Some of the most impactful teachers in low-income neighborhoods could be those who may have spent time behind bars. Their unique perspectives and resilience provide them with the natural resources to teach and guide children who might have been in their same situation growing up. It's a story of success for everyone when people who have just left prison aren't dropped off at a city transit stop with just a "Good luck, kid" as their only support. With proper resources and training, there could be a seamless transition back into society and minority communities. This is what my friend Damon wants to do in our world. He wants to take black men with non-sexual, non-violent crimes and partner them up with schools in the toughest neighborhoods where a male figure is needed who could teach and love these kids and tell them what to do and what not to do from experience.

Amazing program right? I believe so! But even after years of trying, the program has not made its way into our schools because people are afraid. As much good as my friend Damon does in the world as a college professor, best-selling author, and highly sought after keynote speaker, he himself has to check in with a parole officer before he leaves his state. This is something he will be required to do for the rest of his life. That simply isn't fair, but it's his reality. Empathy for those who have different circumstances than us is the only thing that can truly lead us forward. No, I'm not saying that criminals deserve to be free after taking lives and ruining families, but when someone turns the page in their lives, we should acknowledge that and treat them like a human being.

Healing Through Empathy

Merriam-Webster defines the word *empathy* as: the action of understanding, being aware of, being sensitive to, and vicariously experiencing the feelings, thoughts, and experiences of another of either the past or present without having the feelings, thoughts, and experience fully communicated in an objectively explicit manner (Merriam-Webster, 2023).

This isn't to be confused with *sympathy*, which Merriam Webster defines as a feeling of sincere concern for someone who is experiencing something difficult or painful. The biggest difference between the two is that *empathy* involves actively sharing in the person's emotional experience, whereas with *sympathy* you just feel bad for someone else (Merriam-Webster, 2023).

Typically, we find empathy within ourselves when tragedy strikes someone. However, we should also practice empathy before tragedy happens. Take the terrible things that have happened in our past like the tragedy of 9/11 in our country. Because of my age, it's hard for me to have vivid memories of what took place. I was shielded at a young age because of the severity of what happened. Every year around that time, I try to pay my respects like so many others and honor the lives that were lost as well as the people who survived this tragedy, but with their lives shattered.

One of the things that I remember so vividly about this tragedy is the story of so many selfless people coming together in the event called the *Boatlift*. This is the story of people who used their personal boats to evacuate people out of Manhattan. They didn't care what you looked like or who you voted for. They just said, "I want to help" and over 500,000 people were evacuated and saved from Manhattan after hundreds of people used whatever boat they could to help save others. This was the case that happened to my family in the aftermath of the Charleston Church shooting. There were thousands and thousands of people of all races, religions, and nationalities who came together and locked arms to march across the Cooper River Bridge in Charleston, South Carolina. It always seems as though people come together and empathy is shown when tragedy strikes. In a more recent instance, Damar Hamlin, a defensive back for the Buffalo Bills collapsed after experiencing a heart problem during a football game. We immediately saw football players and coaches from both sides kneel down beside him and pray. Millions of others around the world followed this tragedy and donated vast sums of money to Hamlin's charitable organization. I know that tragedy brings people closer, but there needs to be an understanding of others' feelings and heartbreaks even when nothing traumatic/tragic is happening.

By leading with empathy, it is my hope and purpose to encourage you, no matter what issue, concept, or specific person you are grappling with in your mind at this moment, that you might find more peace in creating a safe space for honest discussion and mutual respect. It's easy to get caught up in two sides of one argument, but when the whole world is chiming in, you really owe it to yourself to expand your lens. In this book, I pose various debated ideas and offer you perspectives from both sides with considerations and observations that I hope will prompt healthy, productive conversations towards progress in your own life and community.

We live in a time when it feels as though life is all about what we believe and people could care less about the other side and about learning anything other than that with which they are familiar. This may be a natural inclination, but it is time for us to be intentional about holding ourselves accountable for considering and respecting alternate perspectives and beliefs.

So far in this book, a series of parallel stories have been illustrated in polarizing perspectives. This book is not intended for any group to "switch" to the other "side," but, instead, simply understand why the other side feels as they do and to extend grace and empathy towards a person's personal story and life experience. Perspectives change when we listen to the other side's story and have a better understanding of where someone is coming from. It is when we realize the humanity and commonalities within one another that exist on both sides that real progress can happen. It is natural to fear what we do not know or understand, but there is no better time than today to move forward in the spirit of social and cultural progress, mutual understanding, and–most importantly–unity.

STANCE #6:
CLIMATE CHANGE VS. FAKE NEWS

Robyn's Story

Robyn owns a local greenhouse and has been successful with growing and selling tropical houseplants. She believes there is no conclusive evidence that climate change is happening and that the climate changes that have been measured recently are part of the natural cycle on earth. She believes that climate change might, in fact, be good for the planet and helpful for agriculture. From her perspective, the weather in the last ten years has created a thriving environment for the plants in her nursery. She believes that the media at times can dramatize the reality of scientific discoveries in a way that is counterproductive to life itself. She makes sure to appreciate the life growing in her garden and the natural cycles that occur right before her eyes. "Perhaps the hotter climate is why my plants do so well," she says.

Robyn's Stance

Robyn believes the scale of climate change is not sufficiently significant to take action beyond sensible measures. The economic impact of making substantial cuts in greenhouse gas emissions on the scale suggested by the Intergovernmental Panel on Climate Change (IPCC) and other groups is too large. If the government should be involved in this debate at all, it should invest in local farmers' markets, and promote clean eating, clean production, and building practices She believes the media is feeding "Fake News" to the masses in order to incite fear and garner political support to spend funds that ought to be allocated elsewhere. She doesn't believe that government funding should be spent on issues that have not been proven. To Robyn, the issue of climate change is simply a theory dramatized by big businesses that fund government entities. Although she accepts the existence of climate change, she doesn't think it's as big of a deal as the media tries to tell us it is.

She doesn't believe that making efforts towards preserving nature's resources is wrong. She says that taking aggressive measures might be more harmful than anything else because the funds allotted to said measures would be better suited if they flowed back into the local agricultural industry which would impact a number of issues like American health and wellness from access to sustainably farmed fresh food. When she brings things like this up in discussions with her family members, they think that what she's saying pales in comparison to the impacts of climate change.

David's Story

As a scientist, there is a certain measure of reality that is defined by scientific evidence, especially when it comes to the topic of climate change. In David's research and findings, there is absolutely no reason other than the destructive ways of humanity that have gotten us to this point. He believes that climate change is real and an urgent problem we should be working towards improving every second of our lives.

In his TedTalk, he explained the perspective of an insurance company: "Try to imagine an uninsurable world. Unless we alter things, we cannot afford to operate in an affordable manner" (Ted.com/david/

talks 2007). Meaning, the rate at which humans are destroying the planet is causing irreversible damage and will negatively impact future generations. He says, "This generation has a rendezvous with destiny. We can either work to fix the damage we've done and preserve what we still have, or we can continue living, producing, and consuming in the ways we always have which has gotten us to a point where global temperatures are rising" (Ted.com/david/talks 2007).

David's Stance

David's stance is that climate change is real and anyone who believes something else, is living under a rock and is afraid of reality. He believes that these citizens are a part of the problem. When he votes, the only thing he listens to in elections are the policies and plans that the candidate has for climate change. He often asks the rhetorical question, "Is the Earth heating up or not?"

Glaciers are melting, causing the ocean sea level to rise, impacting the strength of natural disasters and the weather pattern. It is said that the reason for the rise in sea levels (which create larger, more destructive waves and winds) is because of the increase in the earth's temperature, suggesting that the earth will continue to heat up at an increasingly high rate which could result in even more natural disaster and even the extinction of human life.

We are not living in a sustainable way. He believes in the concept of "The Duty of Care" to future generations and that there is no other possible way to promote progress toward a more sustainable future. He believes in government-funded environmental efforts that promote biodiversity and sustainability.

No one can point a finger at someone else for the reason of the earth's climate and the changes scientists have noticed over time. Sustainability is a goal for everyone because we all benefit from its efforts. Instead of getting lost in the argument about which methods of sustainability are most effective in your opinion, define what sustainability is in your life and do that.

We Know Their Stories and Stances–Now What?

Ignorance Is Not Bliss

Everyone grows up with a fear of the unknown; unfortunately for some, that fear develops into a deep-seeded hate. Ignorance, and one's comfort in that, is one of humanity's biggest dividers. False information spreads like wildfire because of the simple notion that we want to see what we believe, perpetuating its existence and truth.

I was recently on a panel with social media experts discussing how we can stop our organizations from partaking in polarizing social media battles. One of the best points was that when you know something's not true, you won't retweet or share it as if it is. Even in my life, I've always respected every faith; I choose to respect everyone's beliefs. With that said, I was ignorant of many aspects of different faiths until I learned about them. It didn't mean that I changed my beliefs, but certain biases and preconceived thoughts that I had were washed away. Now moving forward, if I were to see something about one of the different faiths I learned about and I knew it simply wasn't true, I have the option to address it or not address it, but now I don't have to spread misinformation due to my lack of knowledge.

STANCE #7: GENDER ROLES VS. THE WAGE GAP

Gender roles are perpetuated by the mass media, specifically television advertisements, and certain attitudes about gender roles of men and women specifically affect women negatively in the workplace. There seems to be an illogical assumption from the masses that women are inferior to men because of their physical size, mentality, and "traditional" roles. Many have argued that a woman's most valuable contribution to life is to reproduce and raise those children while supporting her hard-working, breadwinning husband. Should a woman choose to pursue a career while growing a family, she may face judgment that men likely will never experience.

Though there are more women in leadership positions and places of power and decision-making today than in previous generations, there is still a stark wage gap between the salaries of men and women. For many years there was a perspective that, because the man was the sole financial provider in a household, the reason for the pay difference was because the man was looked at as the head of household and wife's job was solely to support the family and perhaps supplement his income.

The reality of the impact of gender stereotypes and the social construct of gender roles through the media's use of ads in conjunction with the social effects of the perception of advertisements on popular television networks is that it indeed reinforces damaging female stereotypes, especially that of the housewife, which translates into how women are viewed–and treated–in the workplace (including, but not limited, to: pay, position, job tasks, paid time off, benefits, etc.)

Many argue that women would not have such a hard time having their voices heard or getting their foot in the door if television advertisements showed women in roles other than the home, repositioning women's body language to power poses instead of bending over/down, using more female voiceovers, and including women in other gender-specific commercials. If practices such as these would change, perhaps society's perception and attitude towards women would shift as well.

Steven's Story

Steven grew up in a small town where nearly everyone's dad went off to work each morning and their moms stayed home with the kids, preparing meals, and cleaning the house for when everyone got home from work and school. His mother took her role as a housewife very seriously, and looks back fondly on all the time she got to spend watching her children grow up. He knew that when he eventually got married, he would want to offer the same level of provision for his wife and kids as his father did for his family.

When Steven met his wife Allie, she agreed that she would like to stay at home while they built their family after they got married. To them, this is a fair division of labor and they both play essential roles in their families. Allie makes sure that their house feels like a home, that the children are well cared for, and that the family gets to enjoy a home-cooked meal each night together.

Because Steven is off at work during the day, Allie still gets time to herself while their kids are at school and uses that free time to get creative and follow her personal passions: art and music. Allie is extremely thankful to be able to live a life that allows her to be home for her family and still pursue the things that fulfill her outside of her marriage and motherhood. Steven has had partners in the past at work who were women with children and beautiful families. Steven had always believed that he was doing most of the work on the projects and when it came to the deadlines he was the one usually working late.

Steven's Stance

Steven feels like it is a man's job to provide for his family and give his wife the option to stay at home and not have to work a corporate job. He understands that being a stay-at-home mom is a full-time job in itself and that he would be doing Allie a disservice by asking her to go back to work. He considers the times when his female colleagues who didn't have this luxury would have to leave work early to pick up sick kids or take extended time off for family affairs. Because he believes that women should get to be home, he often works longer hours than the women on his team so they can get home at a decent time. He is willing to do so, but feels that this is a big reason for the so-called "wage gap" in America. Who gets called when the kids are sick? Mom. Who do the kids want when they're sick? Mom. Who gets that time off to tend to their children whenever it's needed? Mom. So in terms of a wage gap, he feels that men often pick up the slack for women who are in and out of the office tending to their family's needs.

Lindsey's Story

Lindsey graduated from a nationally accredited college with a degree in engineering. She chose this industry because she was raised by parents who stressed the importance of women in the science, technology, engineering, and mathematics (STEM) fields, which are historically male-dominated industries. Lindsey noticed immediately that employers were overlooking her abilities and doubting her ability to contribute in an engineering role. She applied for hundreds of jobs and rarely got called for an interview. When she did, the pay these companies were willing to offer her was essentially an insult. She also noticed the pay scale was not posted on most of these jobs and that the applications required her to indicate her gender.

Lindsey's Stance

Lindsey believes wage gap still exists because of society's collective view of women as second-class citizens in general. Negative stereotypes perpetuated by the media emphasize the false idea that women are less than men and are not capable of the same leadership in the workplace. If this weren't the case, in her opinion, the pay scale would be clearly stated on STEM job postings and the salaries wouldn't be decided based on whether an employee is male or female.

We Know Their Stories and Stances–Now What?

Gender role stereotypes make it difficult for women to be taken seriously in the workplace. Women are limited to an expectation of only being needed in the home, as a caretaker. On the other hand, businesswomen are at times written off as negligent mothers for choosing a career and a family. These gender role stereotypes create a stigma for those who choose to go against that "norm." It is important to note that this housewife image has not been accurate as far back as the 1960s, but that seems to be where the media likes to keep a woman...in the background. Buchanan's studies show that cultural beliefs reproduce inequality, and tying it back to the initial point, that the media creates our cultural beliefs which affect women in the workplace in regard to gender inequality (Buchanan 1965). Part of the solution to gender inequality is equal television advertisement visibility on all major television networks. Attitudes about genders are developed from the media and the only way they can be changed is through the media. The falsely perceived reality must be perceived differently for real change to occur. There must be a mindset shift. A cultural norm must be shattered in order for women to enter the workplace on an equal playing field.

Women have made great strides outside the home and in the workplace since the 1960s, but based on the images sold from popular advertisements, at times it is hard to tell if women have made any progress and impact at all. At the end of the day, women shouldn't be paid less for the same job than their male counterparts. We are still fighting gender stereotypes today, even though we have made great strides in shifting the progress of gender equality.

Navigating The Media You Consume

Knowing how to navigate the media is key to understanding the way existing gender role stereotypes influence both men and women. I know with my daughter coming into this world soon I want her to see herself as a great mother one day (if she wants to have children) *and* the President of the United States if she so chooses, without having to choose between the two.

There is no doubt that the media plants stereotypes in our minds over time that are perpetuated by constant false representation in media advertisements and entertainment shows. From a young age, we consume media that informs us of the world around us in whatever way that may be presented whether true, false, or something in between. In addition, when we are faced with subliminal messaging, it can be hard to navigate where it is taking our minds and how the media we digest can impact our thoughts and behaviors. I think about being black and hearing jokes made about watermelon or fried chicken or maybe even people assuming I couldn't swim. We've heard them all.

Media literacy is imperative as we consume content in a multitude of ways and on a number of different platforms and channels.

The stories we feed our minds determine what we accept as normal, and, oftentimes, as we have seen throughout history with women and minorities in the media, these stereotypes are harmful and socially and politically oppressive.

Women play few diverse roles in advertisements on major television networks and never stray far from the housewife stereotype and what roles a woman should assume in a household. This has perpetuated the issue of gender inequality in the workplace by reinforcing our culture's concept of "a woman's place" being in the home, which undermines women and their capabilities and proven accomplishments outside the home. The gap between the media's image of a woman and reality is surely getting wider as women continue to plow through these stereotypes and challenges in the workplace. The way women are portrayed in the media makes it increasingly difficult for women to break away from the harsh and damaging stereotypes placed on them, especially when the image of these gender roles has been the same since the 1960s. The culture these advertisements have created for society creates a race against time as a working woman in America trying to prove herself. If there were more diversity in the way women are portrayed in the media, society would see and accept more diverse roles for women. If television ads included women assuming leadership roles and the role of provider as opposed to that of the caregiver, single mothers, there wouldn't be such an easy way to justify inequality in the workplace; instead, it would become a cultural norm for women to fulfill these roles as effectively as men. Women wouldn't be chastised for being working mothers if it were a cultural norm for women to work and hold executive positions. The lack of gender diversity in popular television ads perpetuates the false reality of a woman being at her best "in the home" and taking care of the family, leaving little room for her to freely choose a different lifestyle without judgment from others. It is easy for a woman to be praised in America for being a "super mom" caregiver, holding down the fort, cooking, and cleaning, as she welcomes her breadwinning husband home with a hot meal. It is not, however, easy for a woman to choose a successful career path while raising a family and be called out for excellence. This is called the "Working Mother's Shame." Has anyone ever heard of the "Working Dad's Shame"? No, of course not.

The lack of visibility of women in leadership roles in television ads creates a challenge for the woman who aspires to be in the workplace where there appears to be consensus that a man can do more and his work is more valuable than a woman's. A new female stereotype–or, rather, a whole slew of them–must intercept this housewife stereotype that has stuck with us for decades, if not longer, for women to rightfully be granted acknowledgement and credit for accomplishments in their careers. It is important we include people of all generations in these discussions on how media impacts perception when it comes to gender roles.

STANCE #8: SOCIAL MEDIA—THE GOOD VS. THE BAD

The Netflix original movie, *The Social Dilemma,* illustrates the world of social media in a way we might not have considered before (The Social Dilemma, 2020). The film suggests that the dilemma is the fact that all of humanity is at the mercy of a handful of technology designers and programmers who have control over the way billions of people think, act, and live their lives based on the way they engineer social media platforms and their impact on our day-to-day lives. The film calls this group of experts in Silicon Valley "Big Tech," you know, like "Big Brother." That seems like what social media and its impact has become at times with its hold on the thoughts and behavior of millions of followers and subscribers.

Though the engineering of social media platforms might well be cause for our attention and concern, it's important that we realize that fact in an effort to take back control of the images and messages we are consuming. Simple actions like turning off your notifications for social media websites or downloading an app that lets you set a timer on certain platform time usage. Eliminating social media from our lives in any way is virtually impossible (literally). Media and its messaging are all around us at all times: at traffic lights, on the radio, at work, in a doctor's office. When it's so hard to avoid all the noise of the crowd, it is all the more important to practice mindfulness and stay in the present moment. You don't want to have Fear Of Missing Out (FOMO) in your own life because you have your head in your social media apps.

The power of social media can be both a good thing and a bad thing. On the one hand, social media platforms can generate financial support for those in need through GoFundMe or activate change at a local level with petitions on Change.org. While these success stories are wonderful, there are also many dark sides to social media–including the fact that cyberbullying runs rampant.

Natalie's Story

Natalie is a young mother of a two-year-old son, Rex, who has a rare genetic disease that prevents him from going to preschool and building relationships with other children. She shared this news with her co-worker and explained how she hoped to get Rex into a school centered around students with disabilities. The only problem was the price of a private school like this. She would also need to provide all her son's medical devices and medication for the school. Moved by the possibility of giving Natalie's son access to the childhood he deserves and an education in a school built for kids just like him, Natalie's co-worker started a GoFundMe page and posted the link with their story on social media. In less than three months, Natalie's co-worker had raised over twenty thousand dollars to pay for Rex's tuition and resources needed for school. Without the support and gracious donations from strangers and neighbors alike–all over the world–Natalie's son wouldn't be able to grow and learn in an environment that catered to his needs.

Natalie's Stance

Natalie believes that social media has an overall positive influence on society, especially for those struggling financially. The donations received from the GoFundMe were the difference between success and failure for her son whose future was instantly improved when he was accepted into a school that meets him where he is and has teachers and staff who are well-versed in disability education. He is now interacting with children his own age and passing social and educational milestones with flying colors. Attending a school structured for students with disabilities will prepare her son for reality and teach him the skills he needs to advocate for himself in a society built for people who might not be like him. Without the support they received from social media, she would not have been able to afford to place her son at this private school that serves him so well.

Cameron's Story

Cameron was a child with a rare skin disease which made him have spots on his body that were visible to everyone. He attended regular public school and became an easy target for taunting and bullying from other students. One day, a kid named Mike started to make fun of him; despite this fact, the two boys eventually became "friends." Cameron trusted Mike, partly because he did not have many other, if any, friends. One day, he shared his internal thoughts on his sexuality with Mike–who took it upon himself to start and spread a rumor that Cameron was gay. The rumor spread like wildfire and deeply embarrassed Cameron. He wasn't even sure if he was gay, he was just having an honest and vulnerable conversation with someone who he thought of as a friend.

Each night when Cameron would get home from school, he would check what all his classmates were saying on social media. Every day at school got worse and worse with the taunting and poking fun, and eventually a few students started a homo-phobic hate page dedicated to making fun of Cameron. His self-esteem was shot so low and he had no confidence that this situation would get any better. He took his life almost a week later, leaving a note that said, "I thought he was my friend."

Cameron's Stance

Cameron's family believes that social media has a negative impact on society and is harmful to mental health and overall well-being, especially for adolescents. For school-aged kids, cyberbullying has become a deadly epidemic that's been fueled by instant messenger, photo messages, video chats, and social media sites with dedicated hate pages targeting young individuals.

Little did Mike know, his actions were actually criminal. Because he helped create these hate pages and sent such derogatory messages to Cameron in his final days, he was charged with slander and involuntary manslaughter. Many students don't understand the gravity of their words and actions, especially when sent and saved in writing.

We Know Their Stories and Stances–Now What?

Social media can be used for good and bad and how we use it and allow our kids to use it is very important. Not only does cyberbullying harm the victim, but it harms the criminal in a way that might prevent them from ever overcoming the label of "cyberbully." Everything written on the internet can be traced back to an IP address, a specific computer web address that is tagged by its location. Should someone ever be accused of cyberbullying, there are laws that allow law enforcement to track the IP addresses of the hate messages and can then file a search warrant for the location of the computer. This is not something that needs to be taken lightly, and if anything, children must be reminded of the dangers of not thinking before they engage in inappropriate or illegal online behaviors..

With modern technology, bullying is no longer isolated to the playground and the bus stop; in fact, it's even worse than it was ever before because this form of bullying sits in their pockets and follows them home.

I've even seen this firsthand in my life. After speaking to the Houston Texans, the players were inspired by my message and during the season they told me that they would wear my mother's name on their helmet. I was ecstatic and grateful that they would honor my mom in such a way. Weeks went by and the NFL called me, sharing with me that they would post a photo of my mom on the NFL network as well as on their social media. I was super excited to learn that my mom would be remembered during their *Inspire Change* campaign. When the photo was posted to the NFL's Instagram page I quickly went to the comment section to say thank you. Much to my surprise, out of the hundreds of comments that were shown, many of them were hate speech towards my mom. It said things like, "I'm not saying her name" or "Do I have to 'say the name' of every black person that's killed now?" After reading these messages, my heart was broken. I thought to myself: Who in the world could be talking about someone's murdered loved one in this manner? When I went to their social media pages it turned out to be high school and middle school students. Unfortunately, it's not only kids doing this, but so many people we work alongside that use social media as a way to be blatantly rude and/or divisive with the world. If that's you or someone you know, please know that there are real people behind the screen. For you it may be a small matter, but to someone else it could be devastating.

Social media can be used for good and bad, but it is essential for parents to monitor social media usage of their children. The internet is a wide and vast place with tons of different apps like Facebook, Instagram, Twitter, Fanbase, Tik Tok, Snapchat, BeReal, and so many others.. With proper parental controls, site guidance, and human decency, we should be teaching our fellow citizens and our children how to communicate on social media in a way that won't harm them or anyone else today or in the future.

STANCE #9: NATURE VS. NURTURE

Inherent Thought vs. What You've Been Taught

The topic of nature vs. nurture has long been debated. Philosophers like Plato and Socrates believed that certain factors are inborn and occur naturally, regardless of a person's environmental influences. Alternative perspectives like that of John Locke, suggest *tabula rasa*; that the mind begins as a blank slate and everything that we are has been determined by our experiences (Penn State Fanlu Gui 2014). Theorists like John B. Watson believed that people could be trained to do and become anything, regardless of their genetic background or life experiences (Psychology Today 2021).

Nature in this sense refers largely to how a person's genetics influence their personality and behavior, whereas *nurture* refers to an individual's environment (including relationships and experiences) and how these elements have impacted their development.

People with extreme views on this debate are called nativists or empiricists. Nativists take the position that all or most behavior and characteristics are the results of natural inheritance. Empiricists take the position that all or most behaviors are a result of what we have learned and been taught.

This book is written to show empathy for the "other side" and to willingly create a space for open conversation and a place for real understanding. During these times especially, it feels as though life only boils down to what you believe (or think you believe), what you stand for (actions follow thought), and what you have been taught from the beginning (nature/nurture).

Jessica's Story

Jessica is a self-proclaimed nativist. She was born prematurely to a substance-abusing mother whose drug use impacted her fetal development. Because of this, she was diagnosed in elementary school with a significant learning disability which impacted the way she interacted with other students and her level of education. Jessica is convinced that had her mother not used drugs while she was in utero, she would be a lot more successful. She feels as though her mother's decisions have impacted her for her entire life and that she will never be able to overcome this disability she was born with.

Jessica's Stance

Jessica believes that nature is more important than nurture and you're born the way you are and nothing can change that. She believes this because her diagnoses and life challenges could have all been avoided had her mother made alternative decisions prior to getting pregnant and giving birth. If her mother had done so, Jessica believes she would have had an honest chance at life, just like everyone else. Instead, she is stuck struggling with mental processing disorders and has been unable to reach a level of higher education because of her test scores.

Sammy's Story

Sammy grew up with affluent parents who spent most of their time out and about at different social events. Because of this, she spent a lot of time with her nanny, Florence. Sammy's parents would often point out how impressed they were with the fact that she was bilingual and encouraged Florence to teach her more about her Spanish language, heritage, and culture. By the time Sammy was a senior in high school, she was nearly fluent in Florence's native tongue and had even spent time overseas to really indulge herself in the Spanish culture.

Sammy's Stance

Sammy believes that nurture is the most important thing in one's life. She believes that despite great strides in social issues and media policy and representation, movies and shows still continue to portray people of color as subhuman villains, dangerous, and unintelligent. Because of this, Sammy's use of a language other than her native tongue prompted other white kids at her school to question her. Some teachers even tried to call her to the administration for speaking in Spanish "too much." It became evident to Sammy that in her community, where most people only spoke English, seeing and hearing a person like them speak in another language was intimidating and made her teachers feel like she was talking about something she wasn't supposed to.

We Know Their Stories and Stances–Now What?

Both nature and nurture are important variables to the success of someone. The mind is a more powerful tool than most give it credit for. Once we take conscious action and initiative to identify the things about ourselves that stem from either nature or nurture, we can access a part of ourselves we had never imagined. It's all about how you train yourself to think about things, positively or negatively. Think about the concept of abundance versus scarcity. Many folks who experienced the struggles of The Great Depression operate under a scarcity mindset. This is the general notion that you must hold on tight to what you have for fear that when it's gone, it will never be replenished. This negative mindset manifests itself in unhealthy lifestyles that include shopping addictions, hoarding, overeating, or overworking. On the other hand, consider someone who has grown up without ever experiencing life "without." To someone who never wondered where their next meal would come from, food seems abundant. There is and will be enough for them to eat for the rest of time. This creates a relationship dynamic between the individual and their concept of hunger.

Similarly, when we approach a polarizing topic in conversations, the abundant mind and the scarce mind react and interact very differently. I like to divide these two schools of thought by thinking of it as either a growth mindset or a fixed mindset. Are you creating space for new information, thoughts, and opinions? Are you open to rejecting your previous beliefs and changing your behavior should you learn of a new truth? When we reframe our mindset, we can change our thoughts which, in turn, changes our behavior. This involves a willingness to grow and expand our understanding.

"We can find common ground only by moving to higher ground."
–Jim Wallis

I believe that all of us think the way that we do because we were either taught to think that way or we experience something that shapes our thinking. It seems easy enough, but oftentimes we forget that it's either what we are taught or what we experience that shapes us to think the way that we do. An example is my father, Christopher Robin Singleton, or "Big Chris." Big Chris was a huge Cowboys fan once he became an adult from the experience of having amazing players like Deion Sanders and many others on the team during his adulthood which led him to have the tradition of watching Cowboys games on Sundays. Fast forward a decade or so, I'm born and I remember growing up and watching Cowboys games with my father and cheering for them when they won. We'd watch the games on Sunday afternoons and every now and then I could stay up late past my bedtime and watch the Cowboys game on *Monday Night Football*. My father even bought me a small Cowboys pillow football that I'd throw back and forth with him around the house. Do you see why I grew up a Cowboys fan? It was because my father taught me to be that way. We are all taught things at home and, although the lessons may be different, we were all still taught various things that we become as a result of these teachings.

What Do You Believe In?

In this book, you will find many different stories from many different viewpoints. We highlight common points of contention and disagreements on hot-button topics and issues in hopes to shed light on the importance of listening to understand in order to maintain peace.

For just a moment, I want you to stop and just list things you love: Country music? The Browns? The beach? Poetry? Next, I want you to list what you'd say the opposite of each of these things is. Why do you believe in these things? It's a question that we rarely ask ourselves: Why do I even like country music or the Chicago Bears or long walks at night? The answer may be easy for some to figure out and hard for others. I grew up being told by many that if someone was rich that meant that they must have been a crook who made their money off the backs of exploited innocent people. I truly believed this growing up until my perspective changed as an adult when I realized through my own individual success and networking with others that financial freedom in America is not out of the realm of possibility for anyone who is committed to working hard.

It also means that good people can give to great organizations. I'll never forget the first year that my wife and I were able to give $50,000 to charity. This was such a huge accomplishment because, at the age of 25, I had grown up mostly having a goal of merely being able to *make* $50,000; being able to give that much away to charity seemed like something I'd never be able to do. Had I not had a successful financial year, it would have been extremely difficult to do. After meeting many wealthy people, they've told me that the only thing better than making millions of dollars a year is being able to give millions of dollars a year to organizations that need it to do good in the world. The experience changed my entire thought process.

Is there anything you've been taught that you now find to be untrue? I bet the answer is yes. Maybe you were taught that everyone from a certain political party must hate people that look like you or they hate you because of what you believe in. You may hear from a family member that Democrats can't be Christians or that Republicans are all racists. You would probably believe what you've been taught until you experience a friendship with a pastor who says they're a Democrat or you meet a Republican who is black and/or has a black family. The experience changes our mind from what we were taught and hence they are the other reason we believe what we do. Don't hate people because of what they believe because we all usually believe what we do for the same two reasons. Have grace and understanding even if you disagree. When you see people speaking or acting in unacceptable ways, work to teach them otherwise. We were taught to believe the things our parents were taught to believe, who were taught by their parents and their parents, and so on. There is no shame in acknowledging a harmful belief you may have been taught. There is freedom and progress in identifying why you may have thought about something in a certain way and giving yourself permission to hold a new belief surrounding a subject you thought was inarguable. This process is a key component of how we can grow as individuals and form a more unified community.

STANCE #10: PRIVILEGED VS. SELF-MADE

There's nothing better than a story of someone who came from nothing and eventually built an incredible career for themselves. They now give to organizations that have helped them along the way and they pay it forward by helping those who come after them. We call that a "rags to riches" story. Many people believe that these stories aren't really true. In Malcolm Gladwell's bestselling book, *Outliers,* he talks about how many things have to go right in our lives for us to "make it" in the world (Gladwell, 2011). He talks about how luck and timing play a role and how our circumstances definitely have a great impact on our level of success. Some believe that simple hard work and persistence can get the job done and privilege isn't a real thing, but a merely limiting belief that people who don't work hard and want handouts say to those who are successful. These next stories aren't about the rich trust fund college student who has $50 million waiting for him after he graduates, but they will display the concepts of privilege vs being self-made in a way you may not have considered before.

Adam's Story

Adam grew up poor in the middle of nowhere Montana. He was extremely smart and he earned scholarships to attend Duke University for free to complete his undergraduate studies. While he was there he met many people from around the world who had the best laptops, drove expensive cars and were given internships every summer to their fathers' companies. He studied constantly, but frequently felt overwhelmed because he'd never been around so many people prior to attending college. After graduating, he looked all over for jobs, but didn't have any connections and settled for an entry level job at a bank. He saw how his peers who graduated all got great jobs in big cities and used their connections to jump ahead to managerial positions or got to work for household names right out of college. He was upset, knowing that he was smarter and worked harder than so many others, graduating cum laude in his class. Adam believes privilege exists. He has seen instances of opportunity where others with more privilege than himself, got ahead in life. If others could have had the same resources as the person who crossed the finish line before them in the race, maybe they could have crossed the finish line at the same time. Instead, they feel behind those who have almost had an accelerated success story compared to theirs, where they have been working hard to rise in a low-income or low-opportunity situation. They feel that they did not have the same opportunities as their more privileged colleagues.

Adam's Stance

Adam believes privilege definitely exists. He has seen it constantly in instances of opportunity where others with more privilege than he had, got ahead in life. He often thinks if only he could have had the same resources as some of those he graduated with, he'd be in a better position at work with a career trajectory that he'd always dreamed of. Instead, he felt he started behind those who had an accelerated success story because of family connections. He believes that kids in rural areas can be smart, get scholarships to prestigious schools, work hard, and still will lose out on jobs because their families don't have connections like other families do. He believes that kids who grow up with families that have English as their second language must grow up more quickly than others, oftentimes having to serve as translator for mom/dad and getting a job a lot earlier than others because they don't have the privilege and luxury to play sports or go on trips to learn about the world. Ultimately, they do not succeed on the same level as their privileged counterparts due, in large part, to their circumstances.

Norman's Story

Norman is a hard-working blue-collar construction worker who grew up in an underprivileged scenario. He prides himself on having picked himself up by his "bootstraps" in order to forge a path of success for himself and his family. He turned his small carpentry business into a very successful contracting company in a matter of twenty-five years. For ten years of his life he worked six or seven days a week. No partying, no slacking, just "good old fashioned hard work" is what he would call it. His success came from word of mouth about how dependable he was and how great all of his finished projects were. After twenty-five years of working hard on the front lines of his business, he is now solely working in a managerial capacity. He makes $10 million dollars a year, drives the newest pickup truck, and lives in a beautiful 15,000 square foot mansion. He built houses like this for others for years until he was finally able to do it for himself and his family. His children attend private school, but he makes them all work and get jobs to pay for gas and the luxuries they have, because he never had any of that when he was a kid.

Norman's Stance

Norman doesn't believe that privilege is real and it surely doesn't have anything to do with what you can and cannot do in this world. He made it a point to figure out what he wanted for his life and made a plan for how to get there. He worked hard and long hours for years on end until he finally got to a point where his business was highly profitable and successful. He believes that some people need to just do what they need to do to get where they want to be no matter how hard the journey might seem. He thinks, if he can do it then, anybody can do it.

We Know Their Stories and Stances–Now What?

Norman needs to understand that privilege is real and Adam needs to know that so is hard work. Even if you are privileged enough to have certain things that others don't have growing up, it is just as easy to lose it as it is to gain it. Also, there are many instances where you can come from nothing and accomplish a great deal in life. The most important thing is that we all recognize our privilege and work hard whether we have it or not.

Recognizing Your Privilege

A lot of people think of privilege as it relates to money and socioeconomics. While those who have more money than others are certainly in a higher state of privilege than those who are struggling to make ends meet, privilege crosses over into any and every category in someone's life whether they realize it or not. Just because someone might not recognize their privilege does not mean it is nonexistent. A few examples come to mind when I think of these situations.

"Being Born on Second Base"

Have you ever heard that term before? I first heard it at a small conference full of thought leaders, NFL coaches, and aspiring college head coaches where a long-time coach in the state of South Carolina took the stage. He mentioned that some people were born on second base (a term used in baseball) and didn't have to work for some of the opportunities that others had to grind for. He didn't say it in a way that was offensive to those who got to where they are quickly, but rather in a way that made everyone reflect on their own lives. When hearing this it could easily bring me to thinking about the history of our country. Most grandparents in the United States have either experienced segregation or heard directly from their parents about segregation and integration in the United States. It makes me think about how for years it was much easier for a white student to go to college because their grandparents were able to pull equity from a house that appreciated over time and helped fund it, whereas many other ethnic groups weren't allowed to own homes in certain places due to redlining. It made me think of so many other things about how life has always been more fair for certain groups of people than it had for others.

Then I started to think about my own life...Was I born on second base? Compared to my great grandfather who had to work every day since he was in junior high school, of course I was. I have a mother and father that both went to college and were educators. I have an upbringing that was full of pain, but also parents that read to me at night and believed in me. I think I was born on second base just as well. As a matter of fact, most generations will always seem to have it easier than the generation before or at least that's what the older generation will tell themselves. I've always heard that comparison is the killer of joy, but I also believe that comparison can lead to gratitude and understanding whether you were given the new Porsche when you turned sixteen or you had to work a job in college to pay for your apartment. The sheer fact of you not having to worry about things that other people worry about on a daily basis is privilege and could mean you were born on second base and didn't have to hit a double to get there.

Many think much like Norman does, though, I met someone recently in an audience who approached me saying she never thought of herself as living a life of privilege because she grew up in a trailer park. I know many people who think this way and I challenged her by asking her to describe her childhood in the trailer. She began with, "My mom and dad worked so hard for us kids..." and I stopped her right there, respectfully. Could it be that this woman had never once considered the level of privilege that comes along with being raised by two loving parents under one roof? There are people who grew up in the biggest and best houses in the neighborhood but their parents were never around. The deep-seeded wounds that childhood trauma creates can happen to anyone in any circumstance. It's not always about money. She was quiet for a moment and then thanked me for giving her such a positive reframe. She realized how her family dynamic was uniquely consistent compared to others, and they were able to shape her into an emotionally stable and educated individual. Before she walked off, she said to me, "Thanks for helping me recognize my privilege."

STANCE #11:
POLITICAL CORRECTNESS VS. UNFILTERED OPINIONS

It can be argued that "political correctness" (PC) as a term limits the boundaries of discussion, preventing progress on difficult issues facing our world. In a time when we are scared to say the wrong thing, I don't think the idea of being politically correct all the time is something that we should strive for. Now don't get me wrong, we should for sure go out of our way to try to make people feel safe and comfortable, but I do know that language and terminology are always changing and unless you're reading and studying inclusion work daily, you likely won't be able to always say the "politically correct" thing. The goal should be that we create relationships so impactful that if/when we say the "wrong" thing, people in our circle will go to bat for us and they will let others know that people should teach you at that moment instead of canceling you at that moment.

In my life, there've been plenty of times when I've been taught things that I had no idea about and vice versa. A great example of this is a school district I visited in the suburbs of Chicago. As one of the largest districts in the state of Illinois, they know how important it is to have the community rallied behind you. They encourage their principals to be mentored by someone from the community from a different culture who can teach them about cultural differences. If the principal is a white American from West Fargo, North Dakota, but lives and teaches in the inner city, things will likely be different, and having an ally who can teach you the dos and don'ts will allow you to better communicate. This doesn't mean that they need to hang out every weekend with their mentor, but it gives them insights into the way that people who live there are thinking. Even when living in the same city, lives can be totally different, so having a mentor who lives where your kids live is so important.

Wilhelmina's Story

Wilhelmina was named after her grandfather, William. In her culture, it is common for the first-born daughter to be named the feminine version of her father. In this case, William was changed to the female Wilhelmina. The origin of her name is extremely special to her and it's important that people pronounce her name correctly when speaking to her. Having attended grade school in America where English is most people's native tongue, she noticed how difficult it was for teachers and other students to pronounce her name. In her experience, to others, it was "too hard" to say her name so they would nickname her something like "Willie" to get her attention. It might not seem like a big deal to those whose names are self-explanatory or easy to pronounce, but to her, someone who invests her identity in her family and culture, it is a huge sign of disrespect and never made her feel welcomed.

Wilhelmina's Stance

Wilhelmina believes it's easy to make an effort to be politically correct. She thinks that pronouncing someone's name incorrectly is no longer an option after the first try. In the same way we ask people what their pronouns are, we ought to be asking people how to pronounce their names if we are unsure. She believes it is extremely disrespectful to call someone by the wrong name over and over again. Wilhelmina is more than happy to teach people how to correctly pronounce her name, no problem, but her issue lies in the fact that most people don't even bother to ask. They often write her off saying, "Oh your name is Will-something? Right?" And that's not enough for her. She knows if she treated others with this same lack of concern, that it wouldn't go over so well. So why does it happen to her? Asking someone who has a name that is difficult to pronounce how to say it is actually one of the most kind and respectful things someone can do when introduced to someone with a unique name. It is a small but respectful gesture that shows the other person you care about how you address them and that their identity is important to you.

Luke's Story

Luke found himself in hot water after losing a huge advertising client because of something he said to them about their assumed sexuality. Right after the proposal meeting, Luke asked the client if he felt like other advertising and marketing firms avoided creating business strategies and content for him because he was gay. Little did Luke know, this client did not actually identify as gay, and the way he assumed this was extremely insulting to the client, resulting in him cutting ties with the company due to lack of respect.

Luke later found out that his client was bisexual, not gay. He felt like he didn't really understand the difference between the two and suspected that was probably what got him in trouble in the first place. His client wasn't offended because of his question, but he was offended at his blanket assumption. Was it the client's clothes? The way he spoke? The car he drove? Whatever it was, Luke realized that his statement wasn't very "PC," as told to him by one of his "woke" co-workers.

Luke was extremely frustrated at both the client and his colleague at this point. He feels like nowadays, the people in our world are walking on eggshells around each other and people can't say or ask anything without worrying that someone else might get offended. He asked himself and his co-worker: Why was his question so negative? What did it mean that his client was bisexual and why might that have rubbed him the wrong way about working with Luke's company? Most importantly, why was it such a big deal? Luke wasn't suggesting that the client's sexual orientation had anything to do with their prospective business collaboration; in fact, he was genuinely curious on the topic and wanted some insight. He was later fired from his position for continuing to question this client's dismissal of their firm. His co-workers felt like he did not take responsibility for his actions and they feared he might upset and/or offend another client in the future which could result in the company losing thousands of dollars.

Luke's Stance

Luke doesn't believe in constantly trying to be politically correct; he wants to voice his opinion and let others do the same in a way that we can and should learn from each other without people getting so offended. He worries that the culture of political correctness, especially in the workplace, creates hostile and tense environments in which people can't speak their minds freely and honestly. Moving forward, he is still going to ask hard-hitting questions, but he has learned to have more self-awareness when speaking his mind. Not only was this a huge lesson for Luke, but it also prompted him to dig a little deeper to understand the LGBTQIA community and how misidentifying people in these different categories under one umbrella can be harmful. He still doesn't think his question was grounds for getting him fired though.

We Know Their Stories and Stances–Now What?

What it means to be politically correct has been defined in a number of different ways because it is a relatively new discussion as of the 1990s. Britannica, for example, references political correctness (PC) as a term used to refer to language that seems intended to give the least amount of offense, especially when describing groups identified by external markers such as race, gender, culture, or sexual orientation (Encyclopedia Britannica, 2023).

According to the Harvard Business Review, "When people treat their cultural differences—and related conflicts and tensions—as opportunities to gain a more accurate view of themselves, one another, and the situation, trust builds and relationships become stronger" (Meyer, et al, 2019).

The article outlines the following principles as great guidelines for us when making an effort:

- *Pause* to short-circuit the emotion and reflect.
- *Connect* with others in ways that affirm the importance of relationships.
- *Question yourself* to help identify your blind spots and discover what makes you defensive.
- *Get genuine support* that doesn't necessarily validate your point of view but, rather, helps you gain a broader perspective.
- *Shift your mindset* from "*You* need to change" to "What can *I* change?

The fear of speaking in only "safe" PC terms is harmful to the perpetuation of stereotypes and limiting beliefs that surround some of the most argued topics in society today, but speaking without regard for others is harmful and can lead many people with a sour taste in their mouth towards you.

We must have the courage to be honest with ourselves and others in conversations that we have. We need to have compassion for others, and especially ourselves, as we become able to extend grace which leads to understanding and a willingness to connect with those who are not like us. Above all else, we need to learn to be open minded and know that our reality is not the reality of everyone. The most important thing we can do to help is to have relationships with people who can teach us. The following is an example of what can happen is we are oblivious to the surroundings and workplace that we are in:

On the first day of school, Clara, a first-year teacher, was so excited to teach all her students her lesson plan about the beach. Living in the Low-country, this was one of her favorite places to be while she was growing up so it made perfect sense to start the year off with this. She'd been working on it meticulously and it took her two weeks to perfect it. To start class, she opened up the day with a question, "What's your favorite thing to do at the beach?" To her surprise, all of the kids were stumped. They all sat in silence and none of them raised their hands to call out their favorite thing. She then asked the question, "How many of you all have been to the beach before?" Again shocked, only one student raised their hand. She was blown away! She figured that because the beach was less than thirty miles away, surely the kids had been there before, but she was wrong. Many of the kids knew that the beach was close, but had never been there in their 7 or 8 years of living. She had no idea that the students she was teaching lived a different life than she did growing up just minutes down the road.

Imagine if she had a mentor from someone in their school community. That parent or guardian could have explained to her that most kids in that neighborhood don't go to the beach, and she could have made sure to start teaching about the beaches to her students before assuming they all knew. The same is true to making an effort to be politically correct, we won't always be perfect, but we won't get canceled because those who might otherwise get offended, won't. Instead, they will teach you because you have a relationship. It's simple: relationships matter.

Check Your Wedding–*Take a Good Look Around*

If we aren't intentional about creating those relationships with a diverse group of friends and family then everyone at everything we do will look the same and think the same as we do. What good is that and how will you grow?

I remember meeting a set of twins who attended an event I spoke at. They said they had a black friend who was a female and they had been friends since they were kids. She said that she and her sister had been to their wedding twenty-four years earlier and were the only two people who weren't black at the wedding. She said she felt a little uncomfortable and it was the first time in her life that being white wasn't the majority represented at an outing she attended. That day she learned what it must have been like for so many others who constantly feel like they're the only one who looks like them or believes like them somewhere. They said that the same woman got remarried twenty-four years later and after all these years she and her twin sister were still the only two white people out of hundreds in attendance. She didn't say she felt weird about it this time, but she was kind of upset that in twenty-four years the diversity of her friends hadn't changed much. She asked me why I thought that was and the answer was simple. I said, "If we don't go out of our way to create a diverse friend group, then everyone at our weddings and funerals will end up looking just like we do."

Doing the Work: Teaching Unity

"We remember 10% of what we read, 20% of what we hear, 30% of what we see, 50% of what we see and hear, 70% of what we discuss with others, 80% of what we personally experience, 95% of what we teach others."
-Edgar Dale

For us to truly understand what it means to be united, we need to be willing to think with a growth mindset. By now I'm sure you've heard the term because it's essential in creating unity among people with differences. To get the most out of this book we must adopt a learning and inquiring mindset so we, too, can shift our perspectives and work towards a place of understanding and empathy for others.

A person with a growth mindset believes that failure isn't set in stone. They believe that they don't know all the answers. They believe in learning new information and they are inspired by others. They are open to hearing different perspectives and ultimately they are OK with saying that they're wrong about something and open to moving forward to a different opinion once they receive new information.

Generally speaking, it would be nice if leaders in our business community, our schools, and our governments had growth mindsets, but that's not always the case. In an ever-changing world, laws change, needs change, and consumers want change. Growth mindset leaders understand this and don't pretend to know it all. They recruit a diverse staff, they champion diversity of thought, and oftentimes are thriving in life. For example, while facilitating a meeting, a growth mindset leader may leave time for his/her team to chime in with their creativity. The growth mindset leader is constantly learning because they know that the only constant in the world is that it is changing.

On the flip side, a "fixed mindset" person believes that they have all of the answers. They believe that if they can't do something by now, then they'll never be able to do it. The fixed mindset tells them that only their perspective matters. They receive feedback on their performance and it instantly feels like criticism. In order for our society to thrive and grow, its citizens must believe that once new information is presented they can analyze it with an open mind and either change their minds, or simply take the information in and keep their same opinion while knowing this new information.

Fixed mindset leaders may have success, but it's not sustainable because as the world around them moves, they are stuck in their ways. For example, think about all the taxi companies that went out of business because they figured that people wouldn't trust one another enough to get in the back of a stranger's car instead of a taxi. Another example is something that I loved as a young adult: Blockbuster movies. I remember how simple and easy it was to rent a movie or a game and pay the daily rate for it. Innovation and creativity led to this model, but as the world moves, so does innovation. Next was RedBox movies. On my way home at most grocery stores, you no longer had to go to the store, there were small red boxes filled with games and movies you could rent the same you could at Blockbuster, only now it was more convenient for everyone. Innovation didn't stop there, however, in this industry. Now we have Netflix and similar streaming platforms that have eliminated the need to drive anywhere at all to watch a movie or show and we can do all of that from home. Growth mindset people think, "This is the way it is now, but it won't be this way forever." Fixed mindset people think, "This is the way it's always been for me, and I'm not changing my mind on anything."

Recently I was at a conference filled with people in the education field and I met what looked to be an older man with a thick southern accent. When we started talking he told me that he was sixty-seven years old and now works for a school district as a lawyer. He proceeded to tell me that this was his second career; he had run a construction company for many years but his passion for education got him out of that career and into one where he could make an impact on kids. He told me that he has now been on the school board for thirty years for his local school district where he lives. He shared with me that he's grown so much in his thinking over the course of his long life.

He talked about many stories of his adolescence, but one stood out. It was a story of him in sixth grade when integrating our schools in the United States was happening. He told me that there were two sixth grade sections at his school and there were two new black students who were being included in his school. Living in the south my whole life and knowing the history of schools being integrated, it was no surprise when he told me about all of the backlash that the school and the community showed when the students started school. He said many parents wanted to move their kids into a different school, but knowing that integration was happening at many of the other schools as well, most stayed put. That didn't stop them from telling their children that they should never sit next to one of the black kids in class and especially not in the lunchroom. This quickly escalated to many of the kids in the sixth grade making fun of the two black kids and saying to the school staff that they would never eat off the same trays and use the same utensils as the black kids. As he was telling me this, I could see that he wasn't proud of it, but he explained that he thought that never sitting next to one of the black kids and refusing to eat in a cafeteria where black kids also ate was the right thing to do at the time.

He mentioned that as time went on, these feelings subsided and he feels honored that in his town he was able to see integration happen in his class before it happened in many other classrooms in his school and around the country. He told me that he was completely wrong for telling those kids he'd never eat next to them and mentioned that as a twelve-year-old, he was just repeating what his parents were expressing so passionately.

Now at sixty-seven, he is the chair of the board for a school district. The same man who said he'd never eat next to black kids makes decisions for kids of all different skin colors, races, religions and first languages. The thing that changed was that the world around him progressed and after being presented with more information and learning alongside black classmates, he realized that they were just kids–just like he was. He told me he serves on the board with other black people who have that same passion for kids now and shared this story with them. He was embarrassed to do so, but having a growth mindset, he could admit that he was wrong and vowed to make sure kids feel welcomed into their district regardless of their race or background. His story has a great ending, but that's not always the case. There are still school board presidents, teachers, and parents who keep that same fixed mindset and although the world has progressed they may still be thinking that they don't want their kids around others that think/believe/look differently than they do. You see, a growth mindset allows us to admit when we are wrong. It doesn't mean we are bad people; it means we had a fixed mindset and had enough courage to change to a growth mindset. To get the most out of this life, we need to adopt a growth mindset allowing us to see progress and live in a world full of empathy.

I often hear from African American and members of other minorities around the country that the last three years have been both good and bad for them. Good in the sense that they feel like more people care about not being offensive to others and are striving to become anti-racists and more inclusive. Bad in the sense that they feel like they shouldn't have the responsibility of trying to figure out how to fix the problems we are faced with today. I feel the opposite. I feel like this is a great opportunity we have today that my ancestors didn't have in previous generations. For hundreds of years a voice like mine would never have been heard—or if it was heard, it wouldn't have been taken seriously. Now we live in a different time, so when I share my truth, it's not just for me but for the thousands of ancestors in my family who came before me and never had that chance.

Don't Make Assumptions, Look for Understanding

"The problem with making assumptions
is that we believe they are the truth."
—Don Miguel Ruiz

Ancient Toltec knowledge referenced in Don Miguel Ruiz's transformational book, *The Four Agreements* suggests personal freedom can be accomplished in and through the balancing and acting on the following (Ruiz, 1997):

1. Take Nothing Personally: everyone lives in their own version of reality.
2. Be Impeccable with Your Word: keep promises to yourself and others.
3. Always Do Your Best: understanding the best you can do it is variable by day.
4. Don't Make Assumptions: never assume anything;, instead, seek understanding.

I particularly choose to focus on the concept of never making assumptions as it relates to the mission of unity and understanding. You might be asking yourself at this point, "What do assumptions have to do with beliefs and understanding?"

If you catch yourself making an assumption about someone, even if it is quietly to yourself., recognize that thought and notice how it is altering your perspective and dictating your behaviors which directly affect your reality. There are so many arguments and instances of injustice because of unfair assumptions. Unfortunately, when a damaging assumption is held by a large group of people, especially people of influence, it can be tough to recognize its error.

Doing The Work to Change the Way You Think

If you've recognized a thought or series of thoughts in yourself that make you question where they came from, now is a perfect time to dig deeper and to do something I like to call "The Work." It's the hard work that comes with getting to know ourselves on a deeper level and being honest with ourselves.

The goal when doing *The Work* is to overcome your negative and self- limiting beliefs that dictate everything about our lives. When we redirect our thoughts, we begin to exercise the muscle in our being that enacts lasting change in the mind and soul.

Teaching is so important when it comes to this mission of unity. If we aren't actively teaching and re-teaching the people around us in our sphere of influence how to love people and respectfully disagree, hate will spread like wildfire. We have unfortunately seen this unfold throughout history and it seems to have only gotten worse in recent years.

The greatest example of teaching happened to me while I was playing professional baseball in the minor leagues. The minor leagues are a place where baseball players work their butts off to rise up the ranks with the hope of making it to the major league level–in my case with the Chicago Cubs. Being a middle round draft pick with a young family, I learned the value of saving a dollar every place that I could. One of the places that helped me save the most was where I lived. I remember it like it was yesterday, my agent Josh Knipp was phenomenal in getting me the best gear and free places to live. He called me and told me I'd be staying at a place called St. Paul's Retirement Community. When I heard it, I thought it was a joke, but quickly realized that it was serious and I'd be saving money every single month by living there instead of sharing an apartment with someone else.

When I started living there it was filled with elderly people and none of them looked like me, but the beautiful thing is they treated me like I was family to them. After getting a million questions from them during my stay there, I remember making up my mind that they could teach me some things to help me with my mission of unity. I remember interviewing a lady by the name of Esther. She quickly asked me to call her Grandma E instead of Esther and I did. I asked her questions about segregation, her family life, and many other things. After a while, I thought she was getting uncomfortable with the questions I had about race, but it was quite the opposite. She leaned over and said, "Let me show you my great grand babies." I said, of course, and she did. She showed me two little girls, one black and one white and whispered to me that they were eight years old twins. When she said the word "twins," I knew almost instantly that they couldn't be biological twins and asked her how they became twins. She said that her grandson was supposed to have twins and one little girl passed away at birth. They adopted this black baby girl and they were raised together and this is how they became twins. I thought that was beautiful, but the striking thing took place next.

She said, "Let me tell you what they call themselves: Chocolate and Vanilla Ice Cream."

As cute as it was, I asked her, "Why do they call themselves that?"

She looked at me with the biggest smile and said, "Because I taught them that!"

I asked her, "Well Grandma E, why would you teach them to call themselves that?"

With the simplest grin she replied, "I taught them that because I wanted them to know that although they are different on the outside, on the inside where it counts they're both equally sweet."

When she said this to me, of course all I could think about was my mom and the person who murdered her that wasn't taught this. I just kept wishing that he had a teacher, parent, or significant other that could have taught him in this way.

Teaching love and unity is one of the most important things we can do and responsibilities we have when we're working towards a more united world. Either we teach and reteach one another or the information is being learned from somewhere else. Whether you're vanilla, chocolate, or rocky road I challenge you all to teach your family and friends the way Grandma E has done.

Recently I was at a Korean BBQ restaurant with my wife when the waiter started sharing his story. Of course, I'm going to listen to learn about what his experiences have been and to find out if any of mine have been similar. In doing so, I learned about his journey from China to the United States. He told me he was a foreign exchange student from China, but his family was far from wealthy. During our brief conversation, he was teaching me things left and right, including the term *A.B.C.*, which means, "American-Born Chinese." We kept going back and forth and he also taught me the importance of the last name in China, and how that name comes first because it's more important than anything else. He told me every day he wants to honor his family by using the "Lin" name and that's it.

He also taught me that where he was from, if they wanted any kind of soda, they called it a "Coke." So when he arrived from China he went to a pizza place and asked for a "Coke" like he normally would have. Knowing that he actually wanted a Pepsi, all he knew about soda was Coke. Whether it was Fanta, Sierra Mist, or a Coke, he had only learned to call a soda, a Coke. The man at the front desk quickly corrected him and said they only had "Pepsi" products. After a few moments of back and forth, the front desk worker walked to the back to speak with a co-worker, and began laughing at Lin. He told me that he was so humiliated that he stopped trying to speak English for two years. TWO WHOLE YEARS! I was shocked and felt terrible when I heard this. It made me think about so many others who have just shut down and are being made fun of when learning a new language. We should constantly be reminded of the complexity of learning a new language and be courteous to those learning it. He later told me that there was a group of young black teenagers in Brooklyn who inspired him to keep trying to learn the language by not humiliating him when he tried. He used that confidence to become a sushi sous chef where he still was a little reluctant to put what he'd learned into action. Oftentimes as he was preparing sushi, people would come up to him and ask, "Where are you from" or "What's your name?" Lin said he would understand what they were saying, but even though he understood what they were saying, every time he would reply with, "No English," trying to save himself from being humiliated.

This went on for awhile until a man from the south with a thick accent walked in and asked him the same question, "Hey, man, you're doing an awesome job, what's your name?"

Lin answered him like he always did, "No English," he said with a straight face, not making eye contact.

The southern man was persistent and wanted to get to know Lin and asked if he knew any English at all. Lin replied that he knew a little, and the southern man replied, "Well just say what you know, buddy! If you don't know how to say, 'I want to get some food', just say 'I'm hungry' or if you want to get money out of the bank, just say 'bank.'"

He smiled and walked away. Lin took in everything he was saying and it gave him the confidence to just speak and say what he could. Years later Lin is now twenty-eight years old and he works as a general manager at a very successful restaurant chain. In addition to being general manager for several restaurant locations, he also owns two of them.

Lin was lucky to have someone give him the confidence to try again, but I just think about all the others who have had an interaction during which they feel humiliated and they stop trying afterward. You see, we have the power to change someone's life for the better or for the worse, and every interaction that we have with people matters. To you, it may be something small, but to them, it could be huge and keep them from reaching their full potential. Now think about the interactions that you have with people who speak English as their second language. How many times have we heard someone say, "No English" when we try to talk to them? I want us to think about the fact that maybe they don't understand, but maybe they haven't been given the confidence to respond the way that Lin learned to.

Why Our Stories Matter

When we think back to early civilization, there were stories told of many gods. Stories have been told since the beginning of time as a means for information and concepts to live on throughout generations. There was no wide world web to record information for humanity to later refer to. Storytelling is essential for the longevity of humanity. However you choose to identify spiritually, whatever religion you claim as your truth, there is something that unites all who believe in something more. There is even something that unites those who do not believe at all and those who believe with all the faith in the world. So what is it? What is this commonality? And why does it matter? We can trace all major religions back to a few common pillars. Think of these pillars as the golden threads that weave together all of humanity. These are the concepts humans have agreed on for ages. When we teach and challenge ourselves to sift through our disagreements to find the golden thread, we will know peace.

Doing the Work: Be the Change

"Be the change you wish to see in the world."
–Mahatma Gandhi

So now that we've learned peoples' stories behind their stances, how can we keep the momentum going to make this a more united world? We must first be prepared to teach this new perspective to our family members and friends. Running away from the problem or the conversations that need to happen will never lead to success; in fact, that is the perfect recipe for failure.

We Should See Color and We Should See Cultural Differences

Doing the work that I do I've always heard the terms, "I don't see color." Generally when people say this, they think that by saying this it will make them seem as though they aren't prejudiced and they want people to assume they celebrate everyone. The thought process goes like this: "If I treat everyone the same, then I'm doing what I'm supposed to do; thus, people should feel safe because everyone is treated the same." Usually when I hear that, I immediately disagree. I believe we should actually see color and we should see our cultural differences. Our intent shouldn't be to make everyone feel safe because we pretend like they are all the same. Sameness is not the goal. Connection and community is the goal. We can learn to connect with those around us on a deeper level when we explore with them their cultural roots and backgrounds. Through this, we often realize without people even having to tell us specifically why they think and behave in a certain way. I have found in my lifetime that behavior and language is often very cultural, and the friends I've made who have let me into their culture through meals or spiritual gatherings are not all that different from everyone else at their core, but to deny their specific cultural identity would be unproductive. It isn't that we should not see color; we absolutely need to give each and every person of color under the sun the respect and attention they deserve when teaching us about their heritage.

Treating everyone the same will not accomplish the intended goal, despite the best of intentions. I've personally been in plenty of situations when treating everyone the same doesn't work. For example, I speak all across the country and usually when I'm on stage speaking, the crew will set up stages for me and before I even walk in I know I'll have to ask them to add stage lights because of my darker skinned complexion. Now it's nothing to be ashamed of; my parents instilled in me a certain level of joy and confidence I have in my black melanated skin. I'm sure the staff means no harm by not turning on the more stage lights. Most times they have had someone who doesn't look like me stand up there as the speaker and things look great, but because we do indeed look different and have different skin colors I'd need to have the lights brightened to make sure people from all over the room see my face when I present.

One of the most profound examples of why we should recognize our differences is shown in the book, *Outliers* by Malcolm Gladwell (Gladwell, 2008). I mentioned this book earlier in my writing, but I must mention it again, because it is my favorite piece of writing to date. In this book, he points out the fact that different cultures result in different ways we communicate. Even when speaking English together, there are certain things that will be assumed versus things that aren't assumed in other cultures. In some cultures it's extremely disrespectful to question people in positions of authority even if you know something is wrong. In American culture, if someone is wrong, we are more likely to reach out to them to correct them, even if they are someone who is our supervisor. As an education major, we were taught in school that when you're teaching, you should constantly use the CFU Method or "Check For Understanding" to make sure that students understand what you're saying. According to Gladwell, in Asian culture, it is not acceptable for subordinates to question those serving in positions "above" them which led to tragic outcomes. This happened frequently in a stretch of plane crashes when communication wasn't shared urgently because the co-pilot did not feel comfortable questioning the decisions and actions of the supervising pilot.

Culturally we are different in many ways, including the way we communicate, and that is OK. It's actually a beautiful thing to see that in greeting someone there are dozens of ways to do it properly, depending on one's cultural background. We should not only "see" the many different cultures around us, but also celebrate them and learn from them. Through this, we can break down the cultural stereotypes and barriers that hold back our fellow humans in a world that very much still sees in black and white.

Putting This into Action–Unity in Your Own Life

In order to make sustainable change we must take the perspective that we've learned and live out that learning in our everyday lives. My friend Sue Enquist says, "Policies don't change people." She is absolutely correct; policies don't change anything, including people. It is people themselves who change other people by teaching, learning, listening, and loving.

You may be the first one in your family to make the change. Somewhere along the line, someone in our family line has to make a change when it comes to thinking about people who may not think, act, or look like us. It can be tempting to judge because of our past experiences, or the way the world used to be. Or even the way World still is in some cases. But at a certain point, somebody has to make a change. I am reminded of a time I was speaking to a group of parents at a large school district in New Jersey. Many of the parents seemed happy that a young black man was coming to speak to that school district. They talked about the lack of diversity in their teaching population. They talked about the importance of representation and I agreed because I believe it's important for students to see people that look like them when they walk into their classroom.

After we finished my session that day, several parents came up to me and started thanking me for my time with their district. One parent in particular talked about her son and some of the things that he had gone through while in school. This woman was a very educated person, had a wonderful personality, and looked to be a true leader based on our interaction. What happened next took me by surprise. We started talking about our families and I mentioned how I love the fact that my son will have friends that look different from him, sound different from him, and can teach him about different ways of life. I told her that I had to remind my son that he is a young black man, not just Brazilian because of his mother's side of the family. We started talking about sleepovers and this is where I believe some more work needs to be done. She said that she has never and probably will never ever let her son stay at the house of a white family. She said she has tons of friends, but sleepovers at a white family would be too much for her. I disagreed and I told her how maybe it was because I grew up and played baseball and was around people who were different from me all the time, but I told her that we all still have work to do if she feels that way. If she thinks that way, being a black woman in New Jersey, I told her that makes it

OK for a white lady in New Jersey to not allow her child to spend the night at a black family's home as well. She stopped and started to think about what I said and eventually agreed that she still had some work to do because of the assumptions that she was making.

Every time we connect with someone we should make them feel as though they are respected and that they matter. We may think that it's something small so it doesn't matter, but our kids are seeing everything we do and hearing everything we say. We must model the behaviors, words, and attitudes we expect to see in others, especially our young people.

It Takes a Village

You have likely heard the term, "It takes a village to raise a child," meaning that in order to help young people be successful we need people from all different parts of their lives pouring into them to help them get to the finish line.

I believe this sentiment to be true and have seen teachers, coaches, pastors, and many others literally be generational curse-breakers for young people. So, yes, it takes a village to instill hope, self-esteem, and unwavering confidence into young people to inspire them that they can do anything they put their minds to. It takes a village to teach them to be creative and embrace everything about them because it makes them who they are.

I think the same is true for adults though when it comes to living in a united world, we must all be willing to teach one another and be open and vulnerable enough to share our stories with each other. We can't always get our information from one person or one TV show. We must gain knowledge and perspectives from learning about everyone with whom we interact, hearing their stories, empathizing with their situations, and respecting their differences. A village of people who feel safe enough to share their stories has the potential to make you love others better than any book or media source ever can. At the end of our lives, we should all hope that people look at us and say, "The village did a great job with this human being. They gave their best in all that they did, they loved people, and they helped this world move forward to being more loving and united."

Let us never forget that we've all got stances, but behind every stance is a story. Stories told in safe places and listened to with empathy and compassion ignite the change we need for a better world.

Conclusion

We've all heard the question, "Is the glass half empty, or is the glass half full?" Honestly, I'm just thankful there is something in the glass to begin with. When I think about how far we've come as a world, it makes me smile, but I'd be blind to not see how much further we still have to go. I'm grateful that I am still someone who thinks that change for good is still possible. I've learned that it's a blessing to see the world not only for what it is, but also what it could be. I've also learned that the more life we live, the more we all think that the world is set in its ways and change isn't possible. If you think that way, I challenge you to just look back fifty years and then see how different the world is today. If you really want to be amazed, think about the world one hundred years ago, and think about the world one hundred years from now. In many ways, things will be completely changed.

We all must keep imagining what is possible. I think about heroes like Harriet Tubman, Dr. King, or Gandhi and their ability to imagine a better world for all of us. The obstacles in front of them were very real and extremely daunting, yet they still envisioned how different things can be and stayed focused on being the change to make it happen. The world wasn't always the way that it is, but people like them had enough courage to believe that things will be better if we keep working towards it. The world continues to evolve and people do as well. Like Dr. King, I continue to dream. I dream that we will love one another regardless of someone's home address or home language. I dream that people won't be hated because of the political candidate they support, and even when we think nothing alike, I dream that we will not write each other off as an enemy. I dream that everyone realizes we all have stories behind our stances.

I wholeheartedly believe that humanity is at its best when we see the world from the lens of someone else who may not look, think, dress, or speak like us. We owe it to the next generation to love one another and if we disagree, to do it in a respectful manner. The 100 Black Men of America organization has a saying that applies to all of our youth. "What they see is what they will be" (100BlackMen.Org, 2023). Let us lead by example and lead with empathy. The next time you take a stance and you see someone with an opposing view, don't forget they've got a story behind their stance–just like you have a story behind yours.

References

Alliant International University. *What Are the 4 Types of Diversity,* Blog, November 29, 2020.

Baker K, Raney AA. 2007. Equally super? Gender-role stereotyping of superheroes in children's animated programs. Mass Commun. Soc. 10:25–41

Bond BJ. 2016. Fairy godmothers > robots: the influence of televised gender stereotypes and counter-stereotypes on girls' perceptions of STEM. Bull. Sci. Technol. Soc. 36:91–97

Brown, Brene (2012). Daring Greatly. Penguin Random House.

Buchanan, J.M. (1965). "An economic theory of clubs." Economica, 32 (February): 1–14.

Coyne SM, Padilla-Walker L, Holmgren H, Davis E, Collier K, et al. 2018. A meta-analysis of prosocial media on prosocial behavior, aggression, and empathic concern: a multidimensional approach. Dev. Psychol. 54:331–47

Gladwell, Malcom (2011). Outliers. Back Bay Books Publishing.

Gui, Fanlu. Introductory Psychology. *Nature vs. Nurture,* Blog, February 4, 2014.

Hawkins I, Ratan R, Blair D, Fordham J. 2019. The effects of gender role stereotypes in digital learning games on motivation for STEM achievement. J. Sci. Educ. Technol. 28:628–37

Keith, David. "A Critical Look at Geoengineering Against Climate Change." Filmed 2007 at TedSalon, video, https://www.ted.com/talks/david_keith_a_critical_look_at_geoengineering_against_climate_change?language=en

Merriam-Webster. Merriam-Webster. https://www.merriam-webster.com/dictionary/empathy

Merriam-Webster. Merriam-Webster. https://www.merriam-webster.com/dictionary/sympathy

Meyer, E., Khanna, T., & Luc Minguet, E. C. (2019, November 27). When culture doesn't translate. Harvard Business Review. Retrieved April 18, 2023, from https://hbr.org/2015/10/when-culture-doesnt-translate

Moody. 2022, Back the Blue [Video]. YouTube. https://youtu.be/wxAU3WyJMtk

Orlowski, Jeff. (2020). The Social Dilemma [Documentary Film]. Netflix. https://www.netflix.com/title/81254224

Roper, Cynthia, "Political Correctness" Encyclopedia Britannica, 20 March 2023
https://www.britannica.com/topic/political-correctness. Accessed April 10, 2023.

Ruble DN, Martin CL, Berenbaum SA. 2006. Gender development. In Handbook of Child Psychology, Vol. 3: Social, Emotional, and Personality Development, ed. W Damon, R Lerner, pp. 858–932. New York: Wiley. 6th ed.

Ruiz, Miguel (1997). The Four Agreements. Amber-Allen Publishing

Scharrer E, Kim DD, Lin KM, Liu Z. 2006. Working hard or hardly working? Gender, humor, and the performance of domestic chores in television commercials. Mass Commun. Soc. 9:215–38

Sievert, Mike. T- Mobile. *Community Project 10 Million*, Blog, September 21, 2022.

Straub, Kris 2016, July 7, All Houses Matter. Twitter.

Tracey, 2016, November 2, Equity – vs. – Equality.

2023 *Who We Are*. 100 Black Men of America, Inc. https://100blackmen.org/

Acknowledgments

Thank you to all the people who were interviewed and allowed me to use their stories in this book. Someone once said, "Our stories are our stories, but they are not for us." Our stories exist to uplift, encourage, educate, and inspire others. There is nothing more powerful than sharing your truth.

About the Author

From Pain to Purpose

Chris Singleton is an award-winning author and former professional minor league baseball player drafted by the Chicago Cubs. He became a nationally-renowned speaker with a message of resilience, forgiveness, and unity following the loss of his mother in the 2015 Mother Emanuel Church tragedy in Charleston, SC. Chris now shares his message with over 100 organizations annually and his clients include names like Boeing, The Houston Texans, Microsoft, Biogen, Volvo, The Washington Wizards, and over 150,000 students, educators, and administrators across the world.

His children's book, *Different–A Story About Loving Your Neighbor,* was a best seller in its category and has been endorsed by numerous outlets, including The Obama Foundation. Chris' overall mission is to inspire audience members and readers alike with his story of resilience and to unite millions of people with the understanding and belief that, "Love is Stronger Than Hate." Connect with Chris at: chrissingleton.com

More from ConnectEDD Publishing

Since 2015, ConnectEDD has worked to transform education by empowering educators to become better-equipped to teach, learn, and lead. What started as a small company designed to provide professional learning events for educators has grown to include a variety of services to help educators and administrators address essential challenges. ConnectEDD offers instructional and leadership coaching, professional development workshops focusing on a variety of educational topics, a roster of nationally recognized educator associates who possess hands-on knowledge and experience, educational conferences custom-designed to meet the specific needs of schools, districts, and state/national organizations, and ongoing, personalized support, both virtually and onsite. In 2020, ConnectEDD expanded to include publishing services designed to provide busy educators with books and resources consisting of practical information on a wide variety of teaching, learning, and leadership topics. Please visit us online at connecteddpublishing.com or contact us at: info@connecteddpublishing.com

Recent Publications:

Live Your Excellence: Action Guide by Jimmy Casas
Culturize: Action Guide by Jimmy Casas
Daily Inspiration for Educators: Positive Thoughts for Every Day of the Year by Jimmy Casas
Eyes on Culture: Multiply Excellence in Your School by Emily Paschall
Pause. Breathe. Flourish. Living Your Best Life as an Educator by William D. Parker
L.E.A.R.N.E.R. Finding the True, Good, and Beautiful in Education by Marita Diffenbaugh
Educator Reflection Tips Volume II: Refining Our Practice by Jami Fowler-White
Handle With Care: Managing Difficult Situations in Schools with Dignity and *Respect* by Jimmy Casas and Joy Kelly
Disruptive Thinking: Preparing Learners for Their Future by Eric Sheninger
Permission to be Great: Increasing Engagement in Your School by Dan Butler
Daily Inspiration for Educators: Positive Thoughts for Every Day of the Year, *Volume II* by Jimmy Casas
The 6 Literacy Levers: Creating a Community of Readers by Brad Gustafson
The Educator's ATLAS: Your Roadmap to Engagement by Weston Kieschnick
In This Season: Words for the Heart by Todd Nesloney, LaNesha Tabb, Tanner Olson, and Alice Lee
Leading with a Humble Heart: A 40-Day Devotional for Leaders by Zac Bauermaster
Recalibrate the Culture: Our Why...Our Work...Our Values by Jimmy Casas

Creating Curious Classrooms: The Beauty of Questions by Emma Chiappetta
Crafting the Culture: 45 Reflections on What Matters Most by Joe Sanfelippo and Jeffrey Zoul
Improving School Mental Health: The Thriving School Community Solution by Charle Peck and Dr. Cameron Caswell
Building Authenticity: A Blueprint for the Leader Inside You by Todd Nesloney and Tyler Cook
Connecting Through Conversation: A Playbook for Talking with Kids by Erika Bare and Tiffany Burns
The Dream Factory: Designing a Purposeful Life by Mark Trumbo

ConnectEDD
PUBLISHING

www.ingramcontent.com/pod-product-compliance
Lightning Source LLC
Chambersburg PA
CBHW060239030426
42335CB00014B/1536
9798987418420